Mr. Siegel Writes to Washington

Rich Siegel

"We do not have to invade the United States;
we will destroy you from within."

-- Nikita Khrushchev, Chairman Soviet Union

Printed in the United States of America. First Printing, 2019

ISBN: 9781081904241

Book Formatting and Layout:
Elizabeth Klug – https://wordwatcherediting.weebly.com/

DEDICATION

This book is dedicated to David Dennison, banger of porn stars and alter ego of President Donald Trump. You, in your magnificent shabby way, have singlehandedly brought the office of the presidency to a place it has never been -- the gutter.

In addition to the Russian interference in the election of 2016, you have given us nearly a dozen examples of Obstruction of Justice, unimaginable corruption, unabashed violations of the emoluments clause, mind numbing incompetence, allegations of sexual assault and a slew of misspellings that one would simply not expect from a stable genius.

Additionally, you've livened up the National Archive for centuries to come.

Future historians will be treated to lengthy discussions about your sordid affair with Stormy Daniels, star of stage and screen, who has appeared in such classics as: *Snatched, Bikini Kitchen, Trailer Trash Nurses 6, Hot Showers, Pussy Sweat and Porking With Pride 2.*

You've given us these escapades.

And so many more.

Finally, you've given me the inspiration. To take pen to paper. And provide voice to the vitriol that churns in my gut and can only be relieved with legal herbal medicine and the almost daily overconsumption of industrial grade Kentucky bourbon.

Thank you, David Dennison.

TABLE OF CONTEMPT

INTRODUCTION

Before we had officially completed a year into the administration of President Trump -- from here on forward to be addressed as Precedent Shitgibbon, Individual #1 and/or Captain Ouchie Foot -- I began writing letters to Congress.

The reasoning was quite simple.

Any letters written to the White House would go immediately to the circular file. Moreover, with all the layers and gatekeepers at Pennsylvania Avenue there was hardly a chance my missives would land on the barren Resolute Desk in the Oval Office.

Besides, even if it did manage to successfully run the gauntlet, the sentiment and well-hewn fits of rage would go for naught as the utter bawbag we call our POTUS, does not read.

And so I turned my attention to the "leaders" from the Grand Old Party, which is now a Grand New Party, best illustrated not by an elephant but by an aging overfed Yorkshire hog.

The initial effort was haphazard, spurred on by eruptions of frustration and disbelief as in, *"What in god's name is happening to our country? And how can these twatwaffles let him get away with this?"*

Then, as in many of the creative projects I have chosen to pursue, it took on a new life of its own.

Owing in large part to what a colleague and advertising hero, Luke Sullivan, penned on his social media platform. Namely, that each of us has a role to play in this grand experiment we call a democracy. And by that he meant democracy was not simply a spectator sport, it called for participation.

It was at that moment I decided to codify my efforts and take on the task of writing a letter to each and every Republican Senator.

In retrospect, it was an endeavor well suited to my writing style, which is often fueled by tall pots of dark roasted coffee, the occasional vicoden and explosive spates of raw, unrestrained anger.

That is to say it was not without its own challenges.

Contrary to what some readers of my daily blog (roundseventeen.blogspot.com, where these letters first appeared) might think, it's not easy to work up a full head of steam on demand for every Thursday morning blog entry.
There was no small amount of exhaustion at the completion of each letter. Each dispatch felt like running a 100-yard dash. With a 100 lbs. pack on my back.

However, the challenge was not without its own reward.

Prior to this letter writing campaign, I could probably rattle off the names of 6-7 Republican Senators. It's different now. If there were a monetary prize or a giant stuffed teddy bear involved, and with the aid of TruBrain™, the proven memory boosting nootropic, I could spit out the names of all 53 Senators.

And then for good measure, name a few who retired or were voted out in 2018. Or as our president so delicately put it, *"moved on to greener pastures."*

The learning didn't stop there.

Because I took the time to dig into the bios of each senator, I now have a more complete picture of the inner workings of the Upper Chamber. And let me tell you, it's not a pretty picture.

It's an ugly mélange of cronyism, pay-for-play, and shameless, opportunistic pocket lining. All topped with a layer of corruption whose thickness fluctuates, often in conjunction with the rise and fall of the ruble.

As if that were not enough, you will be shocked to discover how many of these worthless blowhards have had run-ins with Johnny Law.

All of which explains why nary a one of them will raise their hand in the defense of our constitution. They know, and now I know, and soon you'll know, that if they ever stood in the way of our Great Muckle Gype, he would commence tapping the keys on his Blackberry with his stubby, vulgarian, and often vengeful fingers.

Each letter will give you a sneak peek into the depravity of the man holding the senatorial office. Correction, it will also clue you in to the five women who also hold the title. Though to be clear they are only women in the strictest chromosomal sense of the word.

None, you will discover, have a sense of pride or duty to their gender and have consistently voted against women's rights whenever they were given the chance. Which has been quite frequent over the past two and a half years.

And that's the other unexpected byproduct of this effort.

As you progress chronologically through the list of dim dotards working at the Russell Senate Office Building, you will witness 30 disgraceful months of the Shitgibbon administration unfold before your eyes. Each letter is a reflection of the current events of the day; the Bret Kavanaugh hearings, the ongoing Mueller Investigation, the Stormy Daniels imbroglio and the nonstop parade of funny, but alarming, Trumpian incompetence.

Now for a little housekeeping.

On January 25, 2018, there were 51 Republicans in the US Senate. That number, as well as the players, changed with the death of John McCain and the midterm elections.

New faces arrived and the number went up to 53. Each has been dutifully addressed.

But wait, there's more.

There are times, and my wife and children will attest to this, when my anger could simply not be contained. To that end, you'll note that I even wrote to Mike Pence, because in the event of a tie in the Senate, the Vice President casts the deciding vote.

And you'll see there's another letter to Joe Manchin, the Democratic Senator from West Virginia who prides himself on bipartisanship. The truth is Joe is nothing more than a DINO, a Democrat in Name Only.

Finally you'll find one last bookending letter to Senate Majority Leader Mitch McConnell.

Because there's no rule that says I can't rage vent twice at that old treasonous bastard.

Similarly, there's nothing that says I can't take the next step in this journey and take on the mammering, earth-vexing, Republican pignuts in the House of Representatives.

With characters like Matt Gaetz, Louie Gohmert, Steven King, and Devin Nunes, that, impossibly, is an even richer target environment.

Chapter 1: Senator Bob Corker
The CorkMeister

1.24.18

Senator Bob Corker
425 Dirksen Senate Office Bldg.
Washington, D.C. 20510

Dear Senator Corker,

Remember months ago, you were stopped on the Senate floor and you forcefully told a reporter, *"...the president is a floundering fishbrained huggermugger."*

Oh, I'm sorry, I paraphrased.

But you did say:

"The president has great difficulty with the truth."

"He debases our country."

"He is not a role model for our children."

Do you remember that, Bobby?

I'd be happy to go to the Google and source it all on the lame stream media, as you alt. right bootlickers like to call it.

Where did that guy go?

Where is this Republican stalwart who finally opened his eyes, and his mouth, and started saying the same sane things, levelheaded Americans have been saying since 2015?

Either you've been gelded by the Child Commander in Chief.

Or, like any good politician you've surveyed the landscape and scoped out a possible opening -- namely the Secretary of State position that will soon be vacant with the imminent firing of Rex "He's a Fucking Moron" Tillerson.

I suspect the answer is a little of both.

Shame on me for believing a United States Senator, from Tennessee no less, would have the wherewithal and fortitude to put country before party.

Shame on me for seeing integrity where there is none.

And shame on me for believing there is a chance that a few good patriots will come to the defense of this once great nation.

From this day forward, you will be known (at least among my 20,000 blog and twitter followers) as Senator Bob Cucker.

Have a nice day.

Best,

Rich Siegel
siegelrich@mac.com
Culver City, CA 90232

Chapter 2: Senator Ron Johnson
The RoJonator

1.25.18

Senator Ron Johnson
328 Hart Senate Office Bldg.
Washington, D.C. 20510

Dear Ron,

Congratulations Ron, you are #2 in my Thursday Thrashing series of letter writing, wherein I contact each of our current 51 Republican Senators and ask why they have done nothing to rid us of the scourge that now sits in the White House. But let's be honest, more often he may be found kicking his golf ball from out of the rough at the misery pit known as Mara Lago.

I'll be quite honest with you, Ronnie, may I call you Ronnie, you weren't even on my radar of senators to joust.

Had things gone to plan, I suspect a white milquetoast guy like you (no offense) would have been letter # 48 or 49. Let's face it, there are so many other high profile clueless canker-blossoms that come in front of you.

But last week, you changed all that.

You vaulted over idiots like Cruz and Cornyn, with your ugly libelous charges against the FBI.

Based on nothing more than Fake News, or something Devin Nunes whispered, you convened a gathering of right wing media and gleefully told your tale about a "Secret Society" of hippy, dippy communist FBI agents determined to turn our country red, Soviet red.

When it turned out to be a joke, you hightailed it back to Wisconsin to bury your head in a wheel of Limburger cheese.

I feel your pain, Ron. And I'm not here to rub any salt in your self-inflicted nationally televised media wound. But if you're hell-bent of uncovering secret societies, I'm here to help.

Please turn your laser-like focus and considerable Senatorial power on the following nefarious organizations (these are real):

The Order of the Peacock Angel -- As the name would imply, this odd religious group are obsessed with peacocks. I mean they really love their peacocks. More importantly, they threaten to debase our Judeo Christian values. Although when people use that term, I'm pretty sure they only mean Christian values. We Jews are generally pretty tolerant and open-minded and tend not to foist our religious nonsense or our inedible jellied gefilte fish on anybody else.

Anyway, Peacocks Ron, Peacocks!

The Bald Knobbers -- They're bald. They wear their coats backwards. And they wear dorky masks. And though I tend to applaud vigilante groups who plug the gaps in our justice system, these underground wannabe cops need to feel the full force of the federal government breathing down their hairy backs.

The Ancient Noble Order of the Gormogons (that's right, I'm working the Google for you, Ron) -- Seems these ne'er-do-wells were formed solely for the purpose of mocking the Freemasons and the Illuminati. They have no charter. No secret code words. They don't even have funny hats. They exist for no other reason than to make fun of other people. They live to pound them to the ground with satire, jeering, sneering, and relentless unmerciful sarcasm.

Actually, I might ask for an application.

Anyway, thanks for listening, Ronnie.

I hope the next time you get to enjoy the national spotlight, it goes better than the last.

Best,

Rich Siegel
siegelrich@mac.com
Culver City, CA 90232

Chapter 3: Senator Jeff Flake
They call me Mr. Flake

2.8.18

Senator Jeff Flake
Senate Russell Office Building #413
Washington, D.C. 20510

Dear Senator Flake,

Another swing and a miss.

Two days ago you stood on the floor of the US Senate to express your outrage (if you can call it that) over the recent remarks of Precedent Shitgibbon. The cameras never panned around to see whom you were addressing, but I know none of your GOP colleagues were in attendance.

So your captive audience included some Georgetown interns (screw Georgetown, Go Syracuse) and a fatigued Chuck Schumer, who was slouched in his chair more focused on his lunch deli meat selection than your passionless pleas. And who can blame him?

This show of yours is old.

And boring.

And from all accounts will not be picked up for next year.

Nor should it. You're all talk. Actually, you're less than all talk.

MR. SIEGEL WRITES TO WASHINGTON

You're an empty suit clinging to the hope that history will somehow judge you better when the Mueller train comes sweeping through and cleans up the massive Republican corruption and complicity.

Here's a clue, it won't.

Fancy words about treason, race baiting and proper presidential manners aside, you've done nothing but enable this sorry sack of maggot-infested flesh.

You voted to buy more yachts and mansions for insurance company executives by siding with Captain Ouchie Foot on the healthcare disaster.

And you were right there, by the side of Senators Cruz, Cornyn and Risch, when it came time to eliminate the estate tax and make permanent cuts for multi-billion dollar corporations while taking Hamburger Helper off the table of Joe Sixpack and Betty Bottle O'Bourbon.

If anyone is treasonous it's you.

You occupy the office of a US Senator.

You go home with the pay of a US Senator.

You get to take the floor posing as a US Senator.

You were elected to represent the people as a US Senator.

But you do none of that.

You're as useless as a mannequin propped up by the CD machines at the Sears in the Phoenix Town and Country Mall, which was shuttered in 2015.

Go away.

Best,

Rich Siegel
siegelrich@mac.com
Culver City, CA 90232

Chapter 4: Senator Bob Corker
Liddle Bobby Corker

2.15.18

Senator Bob Corker
Dirksen Senate Office Building
SD-425
Washington, DC 20510

Dear Senator Corker,

It's been more than a month since we've heard from you. In that time span I have decided to write a letter not only to you, but also to all the GOP miscreants in the US Senate. You, unlike any of your colleagues, managed to merit two letters.

You made quite a stir when you called the President, *"incompetent", "childish", "unstable" and a "fucking moron."* Scratch the last one, which was from Secretary of State Rex Tillerson. I get all you pasty, white Republicans mixed up.

In any case, you've gone radio silent.

It doesn't take a brain surgeon, a rocket scientist or even a stable genius to see why.

There's been a lot of turnover at the White House. According to the failing NY Times turnover is close to 34%, the highest in our nation's recorded history.

Clearly, you're angling for a position in the West Wing.

Good for you.

And your naked ambition.

And your broken moral compass.

Here's a newsflash Cuckster, you're not going to be selected. You'll never be the next Secretary of State.

Why?

Well, let's address the elephant in the room. Considering your painfully obvious lack of height, I should say the miniature elephant in the room.

Precedent Shitgibbon does not like short people. His disdain for Jeff Sessions is quite evident. And, during more turbulent times, he once addressed you as *Liddle Bob Corker*.

Next up, let's talk about your hair, it's very late 80's. And not befitting a US Senator, much less one who is a towering 5 foot 6 inches tall.

I'm guessing you probably don't know many gay guys in Tennessee, but I know people who know other people who get their hair done in West Hollywood and I'm sure we can make something wonderful and fierce happen.

Finally, you have to change your tone of voice.

Maybe I'm not the right guy to be giving career advice, particularly in light of my miserable corporate ladder climbing. But I'm pretty sure I read somewhere that *"you get more bees with honey than you do with vinegar."*

MR. SIEGEL WRITES TO WASHINGTON

It's my understanding that Captain Ouchie Foot is highly susceptible to inordinate flattery. So, If I were you -- and by the way I've been blessed with a healthy dose of integrity, honor and good judgment so I'm glad I'm not -- I would play to his insatiable appetite for praise.

"You're so smart, Mr. President."

"You have the best approval ratings, Mr. President."

"What is that, 9 feet from the hole, that's a gimme, Mr. President."

You get the idea, don't you Corky?

Good luck Bob, I hope your shameless maneuvering pays off and lands you a gig at the White House or as you once referred to it, The Senior Adult Day Care Center.

Best,

Rich Siegel
siegelrich@mac.com
Culver City, CA 90232

Chapter 5: Senator Marco Rubio
The Rube

2.22.18

Senator Marco Rubio
284 Russell Senate Office Building
Washington, DC 20510

Dear Senator Rubio,

About a month ago, I assigned myself the task of handwriting a personal letter to all the Republican Senators, who history will record as this century's Vichy enablers to a rising, terrifying Fascist regime.

That may sound hyperbolic but considering the nepotism, the corruption, the lying, the racism, the cruelty, the treasonous dealings with a foreign adversary and the narcissism gone wild, I don't think it is.

Choosing you for this week's letter was a no-brainer.

I want to call you names and belittle you, if that's possible considering how you've been emasculated by our Commander in Chief.

But I decided the better way was to speak the only language US Republican Senators seem to respect -- money.

Last week, 17 young Floridians, your constituents, were mowed down by a white MAGA cap-wearing murderer with an AR-15, the same kind of assault rifle that the Florida State House Republicans, your colleagues in crime, refused to ban.

Or even debate.

Almost all of those killed were students, meaning they had the rest of their lives in front of them. So let's do a little speculative Morbid Math, shall we Marco?

Let's say the average age of each victim was 15 years old.

Let's also assume that each of these bright, healthy promising 15-year-old kids would have lived to 80.

$80 - 15 = 65$ years.

These dead students were robbed of 65 years of life. Or, as Republicans like to think of it, revenue earning potential.

For the sake of this revolting argument, let's say some of those kids would have gone on to become doctors, lawyers, Wall Street brokers as well as a healthy mix of teachers, fireman and office janitors.

So let's assume the average yearly income of these kids -- let's remind ourselves they were kids -- would have been a modest $100,000 a year.

Now comes the interesting part, by which I mean the disgusting part:

17 victims X 65 years of earning potential

1105 years of lost earnings

We're not done, Liddle Marco.

RICH SIEGEL

1105 Y.L.E. X $100,000 average salary (and this number could
easily be doubled)

That's $110,500,000 of accumulative wealth that was not earned,
that was not added to our oh-so-precious GDP, that was not tallied in
the Republican effort to Make America Great Again.

Over the course of your worthless career, you've accepted
$3,303,355 from the NRA.

If you'll permit me one last calculation, if we disregard the
heartache, the humanity and the unspeakable loss of life that clearly
means nothing to you and your NRA taskmasters, you have
personally cost us, Floridians and the US taxpayer, roughly $107
million dollars.

So you're not only a piss poor excuse for a human being, you're an
incompetent, financially irresponsible Republican.

Best regards,

Rich Siegel
siegelrich@mac.com
Culver City, CA 90232

Chapter 6: Senator Chuck Grassley
The Lawn Jockey

2/28/18

Senator Chuck Grassley
135 Hart Senate Office Building.
Washington, DC 20510

Dear Senator Grassley,

You are a useless old fuck.

I hate to start out using coarse language and pejoratives that no United States Senator wants to hear, but useless was the best and only word that came to mind.

Let me back the train up and explain that I have assigned myself the task of handwriting letters to each and every one of our Republican US Senators, men and women like you, who have been complicit in the immoral, illegal and very likely traitorous administration of one witless Precedent Shitgibbon.

Again, I apologize for the language, but that man-child is witless.

Today is your turn in the barrel.

Why, you may ask?

Because we have reached a pivotal point in the ongoing Russian investigation. Rick Gates has just flipped and is now providing evidence against Paul Manafort. They were both operating as foreign agents of Ukraine and, by proxy, Russia. And they were both laundering dirty money for thuggish oligarchs.

Even if we were to assume that Captain Ouchie Foot had nothing to do with these criminal shenanigans, the fact remains that he hired Manafort and Gates, as well as Papadopoulos and General Flynn. So despite his constant pleas for extreme vetting, he did no vetting and let these admitted foreign agents into the inner sanctum of our government.

That alone should have you screaming from the rafters. You know after you empty your Senate bedpan.

Now, let's look at an even worse and more probable scenario.

I believe Mr. Mueller will present copious evidence that your president was not an oblivious bystander to all this Russian financial fuckery.

I believe that Mueller, a lifelong Republican and war hero, whose integrity is beyond reproach (particularly from lowlifes Devin Nunes and Matt Gaetz), will confirm the charges in the Steele Dossier.

I believe that Americans will soon be talking about Bayrock and Felix Sater. And that they will be household names just as Haldeman and Ehrlichman were some 40 years ago.

MR. SIEGEL WRITES TO WASHINGTON

I believe the president's refusal to issue Russian sanctions, to take any meaningful preventative measures on our next election and to constantly deflect to Hillary Clinton is a red flag warning to any thinking, rational warm blooded American patriot.

Which you, clearly are not.

Because in light of all this, you choose to spin your wheels on the finer technical points of the FISA application to surveil Carter Page!!!

You're as useless as the forward gears on a French tank.

Best regards,

Rich Siegel
siegelrich@mac.com
Culver City, CA 90232

Chapter 7: Senator Mitch McConnell
Mitch Malignant

3.8.18

Senator Mitch McConnell
317 Russell Senate Office Building,
Washington, DC 205100001

Dear Senator McConnell,

A little more than a month ago I embarked on a mission to write to each of our Republican US Senators and offer them my personal review of their performance.
This is now the 6th letter of its kind.

With you being the ranking majority Senator, you'd think you would have been the first to receive a letter. That honor went to Bob Corker.

In fact, perhaps due to my early senility or perhaps due to the hot lava like rage I feel towards your Tennessee crony, I've actually penned TWO letters to Corky, who flips and flops more than an oxygen-starved mackerel on the deck of an Alaska fishing boat.

A long-winded way of saying, Mitch, you just don't merit my respect.

Truth be told, I had given serious thought to writing all 51 letters and purposely *not* writing to you -- the Merrick Garland treatment if you will.

MR. SIEGEL WRITES TO WASHINGTON

But, here we are, so permit me to unload on the heinous positions
you have taken on the pressing issues of the day.

On Russian election interference, you stated...oh wait you haven't
stated anything.

On the House Intel Committee debacle, uh...again nothing.

On Stormy Daniels, nothing.

On the breakdown of DACA talks, nothing.

On the recent Florida school shootings, nothing.

On gun reform, nothing. (That's not true, you mentioned gun control
and then said bank reform was much more important.)
On the Rob Porter wife beating, nothing.

On the porous WH security clearance passes, nothing.

On the president's refusal to issue Russian sanctions, nothing.

On shithole countries, nothing.

On the president's personal attacks on fellow Senator John McCain,
nothing.

On Kellyanne Conway's violation of the Hatch Act, nothing.

On the bogus Devin Nunes Memo, nothing.

On Charlottesville, nothing.

On the failed rescue of Puerto Rico, nothing.

I'm sure you are aware of the *testidunatal* meme concerning your
indifference to such suffering.

Personally, I find the whole turtle sticking its head in its shell to be tired and hackneyed. Moreover, it's wrong. Because it connotes a moving, breathing organism that still possesses life.

But, like ethics, morals and sense of duty to country, you have none.

I prefer to think of you not as some kind of decrepit terrapin but as a large, muddied sedimentary boulder pressing down on the neck of America. Suffocating the country with nothing more but the unmoving forces of gravity, until the lifeblood of democracy and liberty no longer flow freely, leaving nothing but the dried up corpse of a once great nation.

That'll be your legacy, Mitch.

Have a great day, Senator.

Rich Siegel
siegelrich@mac.com
Culver City, CA 90232

Chapter 8: Senator Cory Gardner
Herb

3.14.18

Senator Cory Gardner
B40B Dirksen Senate Office Building
Washington, DC 20510

Dear Senator Gardner,

Today, I find myself in the unusual position of heaping a little praise on a Republican Senator. For the past two months that has not been the case.

You see, I have started a Thursday Thrashing series for readers of my blog roundseventeen.blogspot.com. I invite you to scan through the past two months and witness the abuse I have rained down on your colleagues, including Flake, Corker, McConnell and that tin foil hat-wearing Ron Johnson.

But last week, you did what few US Senators dared to do. You stood up to the administration. You spoke out in favor of a more liberal, pragmatic approach to marijuana. In essence, you told our perjuring little Attorney General Jeff Sessions, to chillax and roll himself a phat one. Good on you, Cory.

But before you go running down the hallway and start waving this letter in Senator Corker's face, let's do a little chilling of our own.

Because it's my understanding that when presented with a reasonable gun control bill that included the NICS Fix (National Instant

Criminal Background Check System), you parked your fat Colorado
ass in front of it, like a bloated steer napping on a railroad track.

I don't know what I find more repulsive. Your objection to
instituting universal background checks for gun ownership and thus
preventing loonies, convicted murderers and terrorists on the No Fly
List from obtaining weapons of massive flesh destruction.

Or, the fact that your hesitance stems from some arcane, twisted
reading of the US Constitution. *"We have to be very careful not to
trample the inalienable rights of law abiding citizens."*

It's 2018, Cory. We're not talking about single action muskets. We're
talking about high capacity semi-automatic assault rifles.
I'm a law-abiding citizen and I don't want to have to look over my
shoulder every time I step into a school, a mall, a synagogue or even
Dodger Stadium. That's a clear violation of my inalienable rights.

When did we get so high and mighty about looking into people's
background before we allow them to make a major purchase? Last
week, I bought myself a pre-owned car at an Audi dealership in
Ontario, CA. Since they were offering attractive rates, I did the
financing through their office. The process took me more than two
hours.

And it included some very rigorous investigation. Before handing
me the keys, they wanted to know:

* My social security number

* My income

* My mortgage payments

* My shoe size

MR. SIEGEL WRITES TO WASHINGTON

And guess what? I gladly provided all the info. And did so without whipping out my pocket Constitution or checking to see if my *Habeas Corpus* had been unlawfully trampled upon. Because I wanted the car. And because I had nothing to hide.

Isn't that the same logic used by law and order Republicans to justify the inner city stop-and-frisk procedure? If I were the Doubting Thomas type, I'd say there's a little hypocrisy going on here, Cory. I might even suggest it has something to do with the color of one's skin.

Normally, I end these letters with a barrage of insults and a volcano like eruption of anger. But because my daughter goes to the University of Colorado. And because I'm still enjoying the afterglow of my new car purchase. I'm going to pass.

BTW, for handing over all my info and for being so cooperative, the Audi dealership threw in free floor mats and coupons for 10 free car washes.

Maybe the gun folks could consider something similar.

Best,

Rich Siegel
siegelrich@mac.com
Culver City, CA 90232

Chapter 9: Senator Dean Heller
Heller, the Vote Seller

3.22.18

Senator Dean Heller
324 Hart Senate Office Building
Washington, DC 20510

Dear Senator Heller,

Can I be frank with you?

Until Precedent Shitgibbon singled you out last year for your
possible NO vote of the ObamaCare repeal and replace proposal, I
had never heard of you.

I'm guessing most Nevadans, in perpetual search of hookers, high
paying slot machines and $7.99 breakfast buffets, had never heard of
you either.

Let's face it, you've hardly established yourself as that "unstoppable
legislative force from Castro Valley."

Moreover, your reputation as a wispy empty suit was only reinforced
when you sat next to Captain Ouchie Foot and donned a sheepish
grin while he humiliated you before your colleagues and a nation of
onlookers who collectively thought...

"Who's that dipshit?" (No offense)

And yet for all that non-noteworthy anonymity, you sir, are #8 in my

MR. SIEGEL WRITES TO WASHINGTON

Thursday Thrashing series of letters to all 51 Republican US Senators.

A person of normal intelligence might be asking, *"What have I done to deserve such an honor?"* But I think we can all agree you're hardly a person of normal intelligence.

The fact that you are running for re-election is testament to that.

Speaking of the upcoming Nevada Senatorial race, it's my understanding that you will be facing off against Democrat Jacky Rosen. Naturally I'll be pulling for her. Because as one Internet meme put it, "any vote for a Democrat is a vote for a future jury panel on the Trump impeachment."

But I'm not just willing to write a check and voice my support for Ms. Rosen, I want to do more. I have to do more.
Because, if I can be frank again, people like you are destroying this country; adding to our national debt, trashing social advancements, fueling tribalism, supercharging corruption and desecrating our national institutions like the free press and the Department of Justice.

So, I'm throwing a rusty monkey wrench into the democracy machine.

And by that I mean I'm hoping to siphon off Republican voters, who would vote for you, by throwing another, more qualified, more dignified Republican candidate into the mix.

Meet Bull Feces, a 50 lbs. bag of Grade A manure sold on Amazon.com.

You may scoff and think you can't run a 50 lbs. bag of manure for the US Senate. I would remind you of that old legal maxim, *"in today's litigious society, you can sue a ham sandwich."*

Additionally, we live in a special time when technology makes it

25

possible to create and design an entire political campaign right from the comfort of our desktop.

I am more than willing to apply my 25 years of marketing expertise to this endeavor.

If I can secure 1000 write in votes for Bull Feces in the November election -- that's 1000 votes that won't go to you -- I will consider that a victory.

There is an upside to all this, Dean.

You see while I doubt you can stand toe to toe with Ms. Jacky Rosen in a one on one debate. I'm betting that you have the skill set and the intellectual firepower to hold your own with the new Republican challenger, a 50 lbs. bag of manure.

Or, in the parlance of Nevadan's, I have you at even money with Bull Feces.

Best,

Rich Siegel
siegelrich@mac.com
Culver City, CA 90232

Chapter 10: Senator Susan Collins
The Shame of Maine

3.29.18

Senator Susan Collins
413 Dirksen Senate Office Building
Washington, DC 20510

Dear Senator Collins,

You have my sympathy.

And believe me I don't say that to every Republican United States Senator. In fact, since I started my Thursday Thrashing series, wherein I write a personal letter to each senator -- it's now Week #9 - - I haven't said that to any.

But I sense you're different.

After all, you did vote NO on the bill to kill ObamaCare and showed a momentary flash of common sense not known to your current colleagues.

Of course, that was short-lived, like that time Precedent Shitgibbon strung together a complete sentence. Because when the Tax Scam Bill came around, you know the one that gives tax breaks to our wealthiest oligarchs and adds 1.4 trillion dollars to our national debt, you lined up at the trough like a fat guy at an all you can eat ice cream sundae bar.

But your YES vote was more noteworthy than others. Because in exchange for your vote, Mitch McConnell promised an insurance stabilization bill that would help your Maine constituents.

You can pin that insurance stabilization bill up on the Wall that will never get built.

By Mexicans who will never pay for it.

In the words of Malcolm X (he's a black guy, you've probably never seen or heard of him)...

"You got hoodwinked. You've been bamboozled. Old Turtlehead had you for breakfast."

So after this public humiliation, where does that leave you, Susie? Mitch made you his bitch. And Captain Ouchie Foot, will forever be giving you the side-eye. Which makes you a woman without a country.

But it doesn't have to be that way.

There's a Blue Wave coming.

We saw it in Alabama. And most recently in Pennsylvania. And that wave will only magnify in intensity as we sort through the unsavory details of our president's dilly-dallying with Stormy Daniels, The 7,381st Lady, if you will.

Besides, why would you want to be associated, even marginally, with the party that is synonymous with racism, misogyny, corruption, federal election tampering and oh, here's the latest one, hatefully victimizing teens who were already victims of a Florida mass shooting?

MR. SIEGEL WRITES TO WASHINGTON

The writing is on the wall.

The iceberg is straight ahead.

And the timing couldn't be better.

The way to get out is to get in with the Democrats.

Welcome aboard, Suze.

Best,

Rich Siegel
siegelrich@mac.com
Culver City, CA

Chapter 11: Senator Ted Cruz
(You don't get a nickname, what could be worse than Ted Cruz?)

4.5.18

Senator Ted Cruz
Russell Senate Office Bldg. 404
Washington, DC 20510

Dear Senator Cruz,

Yesterday it was reported that your Democratic opponent in this year's Senate race, Beto O'Rourke raised $6.7 million in campaign funds. That's a lot of cash.

With money like that you could buy a $31,000 dinette set. Or a $141,000 door. Or even charter military jets to whisk you around the world.

But Beto, has different plans. He's going to use that money to unseat your sorry ass. If only that would've happened earlier, I wouldn't be on this current kick to hand write letters to all 51 of the incompetent, and often traitorous, Republican US Senators. I'd only have to write to 50.

I'm not even going to attempt to insult you. I'm afraid anything I offer in this arena will pale in comparison to the many thousands of pointed barbs hurled in your putrid direction.

Besides, I know there's no way I could top your former Senate colleague, Al Franken, who famously said, *"I like Ted Cruz more than most people in the Senate Chamber. And...I hate Ted Cruz."*

I can't do better than that. But here's what I can do.

As of November 7th, 2018, it's a safe bet you will find yourself unemployed. Chances are you've socked away some money made from influence peddling or some insider trading into a bank in the Cayman Islands, though my understanding is Cyprus with its various ties to Russian oligarchs is the preferred choice of today's Republicans.

Still, it's nice to wake up in the morning and have a purpose.

Mine for instance is calling out the endless stream of horsecockery you and your party and your flap dragon of a president foist upon this nation, day after punishing day.

So I've taken the liberty of seeking out employment opportunities for one Mr. Theodore Cruz in the greater Houston area. Here are some real unfilled positions in your area:

Nursing Home Magician, Sunrise of Cinco Ranch Nursing Home-- Currently seeking a part time magician to entertain our guests three nights a week. Prefer magician with excellent sleight of hand work. Must be proficient at juggling. And have loud, clear speaking voice. No flammables, please.

Fruit Freshener, Hung Dong Supermarket-- Located right outside Stuebner Center, Hung Dong is a local favorite. This is a full time position that requires a keen eye, as you will be responsible for maintaining our fruits and vegetable display. Making sure they always look farm-fresh with water dew and proper color coordination. Perfect job for a recent retiree.

RICH SIEGEL

Cat Holder Downer (from Craig's List)-- I'm new to town and need someone to help me for about half an hour while I give my rockin' awesome cat a haircut. I don't want to pay a groomer $75 and don't want to stress my fantastic feline out by taking him somewhere he's not comfortable. He is very docile and does not mind this procedure; it's just a two man job that I'm short a reliable person to operate. All I need you to do is 1) Be cool 2) Dig cats 3) Hold my cat for half an hour. He 1) Rawks 2) Will not bite, scratch, urinate, defecate and/or molest, harry and/or pillage your forearm region. He will 1) lick 2) head butt and/or 3) give aforementioned area loving attention.

This needs to be done at my apartment and I will compensate you with beer, good music, stimulating conversation & $10. I will not monetarily compensate any colleagues you bring; however, said cohorts may help themselves to one of the following options 1) one alcoholic beverage & one snack 2) two non-alcoholic beverages & one snack 3) unlimited ice cold water & two snacks. Also, you may choose to watch television and/or listen to my massive collection of vintage and contemporary vinyl collection while grooming is being performed.

The good news Senator is that should you decide to accept any of these positions you will receive more respect and more admiration than you had at your previous position. Good luck out there.

Best,

Rich Siegel
Culver City, CA
siegelrich@mac.com

32

Chapter 12: Senator Rand Paul
Señor Flip Flop

4.25.18

Senator Rand Paul
167 Russell Senate Building
Washington DC, 20510

Dear Senator Paul,

You know what I love about Libertarians, Rand?

Nothing.

It's been my observation that they talk tough, "gotta cut spending", "gotta make government small", "gotta restore moral clarity to our nation", but when the rubber hits the government-funded roads, they fold like cheap, thin crust pizza.

Let me back the government-purchased truck up and explain that I have made it my mission to write letters to each of our 51 US Republican Senators. Not that it will accomplish anything (a perfect metaphor for the Senate if there ever was one), but more to serve as a venting mechanism for my growing outrage.

You sir, are letter #11.

And as you might expect, after this week's Kentucky Two Step before the TV cameras, you were the easy choice.

RICH SIEGEL

It was just a week ago when you lectured Secretary of State Mike Pompeo (then only a candidate) on our oh-so-precious Constitution.

"Mr. Pompeo, the President does not have the authority to bomb Assad's forces. Our founding fathers gave the authority to Congress, and actually they're uniformly opposed to the executive branch having that power."

Those were your eloquent but hollow words. You followed that up with a very public denouncement of Mr. Pompeo and a pompous pledge not to confirm him.

Then, I must assume, Precedent Shitgibbon got you on the phone and promised you a lifetime golf membership at Mara Lago, including complimentary tees and golf club scrubbing, because a few days later, you had pocketed your pocket Constitution and were confidently voting this torture-happy blowhard into one of the most powerful positions on the planet.

Nice job, Rand.

But you know what? I understand a change of opinion. And a flip flop.

In fact, I wish the judge who settled the recent dispute between you and your cantankerous neighbor would reconsider his ruling.

"I know I initially ruled against the Senator's neighbor. He had no right store his ugly brush pile of yard junk on Mr. Rand Paul's property. I know I accepted the neighbor's guilty plea for arguing with Mr. Paul and then attacking him, pulling his curly hair and kicking his ribs.

MR. SIEGEL WRITES TO WASHINGTON

But I have re-reviewed my findings and wish to reverse them.

For no other reason than the Senator is a wishy washy weenie with the backbone of a garden snake and the fortitude of a campground marshmallow. Plus, and I believe this trumps all, Rand Paul's got a face you just want to punch."

Best,

Rich Siegel
siegelrich@mac.com
Culver City, CA 90232

Chapter 13: Senator John Cornyn
Cornholio

5.10.18

Senator Cornyn
517 Hart Senate Office Bldg.
Washington DC, 20510

Dear Senator Cornholio,

I'm sorry. I shouldn't refer to you like that.

It's juvenile. It's base.

And it's simply not fitting for a United States Senator. You'd think that in my mission to write letters to each and every one of the Republican US Senators (you're #12), I'd have gotten past those kind of sophomoric hijinks.

But, apparently I have not.

Plus, it doesn't help that every time you appear on TV, whether it's to fawn over Precedent Shitgibbon or to cower before Precedent Shitgibbon or even just to roll over on your belly and play submissive to Precedent Shitgibbon, I turn to my wife and refer to you as Senator Cornholio.

Again, I apologize.

MR. SIEGEL WRITES TO WASHINGTON

Let's get to more meaty matters and talk about your significant achievements during your 16-year tenure and your current position as Senate Majority Whip.

(DRAMATIC PAUSE TO INDICATE RIGOROUS RESEARCH)

I see you haven't really done much. An indication that like your useless Senate cronies, you have found the perfect vocation in life.

But at least you look like a US Senator.

There can be no denying that with your towering height, athletic physique and fine silvery hair, you are quite photogenic.

Add to that, those gleaming white teeth and I think it's safe to say that you look like you came right out of Central Casting, a favorite trope of Precedent Shitgibbon.

In fact, the more I think about you, Senator Cornholio, the more it dawns on me that you are doppelganger for Senator Geary, who made his debut appearance at the beginning of Godfather II.

You remember that scene don't you?

The resemblance is a little uncanny, wouldn't you agree?

I'm sorry I had to equate you with such an oily, sticky-palmed greedy bastard like Senator Geary, who stupidly tried to extort Michael Corleone and the Mafia for $250,000.

Furthermore, and let me make this point perfectly clear, I am in no way insinuating that the mob, Italian, Russian or otherwise, bailed your ass out of a jam when they found you in a brothel, naked and bloodied, and consorting with a 16 year old, heroin-addicted prostitute.
I'm not saying that happened at all.

I'm saying that I wouldn't be surprised if it ever does.

Best,

Rich Siegel
siegelrich@mac.com
Culver City, CA 90232

Chapter 14: Senator John Barasso
Mahoney

5.17.18

Senator John Barasso
307 Dirksen Senate Office Building
Washington, DC 20510

Dear Senator Barasso,

It's safe to say, Senator Barasso, that of all the 51 Republican US Senators (I'm penning handwritten letters to all of them) you are my favorite.

You are my favorite because you clearly subscribe to the theory that Republican Senators are like children and should be seen, not heard.

In fact, during the past two years where I have been following your "career", I have yet to hear you utter one word. In essence, making you the harmless skin tag on the back of Mitch McConnell's flappy neck.

For those unacquainted -- and I suspect that number runs in the millions -- I suggest a Senator Barasso Image Search on Google.

It can hardly be an accident that every time Mitch spots an open microphone and a TV camera, you are there at his side.

Stoic.

Silent.

And dare I say, useless.

By the way, if you wanted to use that as your next re-election slogan, it's yours for the taking.

Senator John Barasso.
Stoic. Silent. And Useless.

I suspect that platform would appeal to the mouth breathers of Wyoming, where you currently serve. In fact, if your Wikipedia page is correct you started serving Wyomingites in 2002, when you were elected and ran un-opposed.

You won again in 2006. And again you were unopposed.

One can only conclude that the good folks in Wyoming will go out of their way, not to get in the way of yours. And they couldn't be happier with your legendary inaction.

You, sir, are the incarnation of small government. A Republican wet dream, draped in a suit purchased off the rack at the Cheyenne Big & Tall.

Your lack of leadership, inability to move the ball forward and remarkable capacity for standing behind other ineffectual white men in poorly tailored suits serves to inspire others, others who dream of wielding great power while sucking freely on the teat of the taxpayer revenue base.

MR. SIEGEL WRITES TO WASHINGTON

I salute you Senator John Barasso.

You saw the Peter Principle, and unwilling to accept it at face value, have come to redefine it for generations of Congressional underachievers to come.

Best,

Rich Siegel
siegelrich@mac.com
Culver City, CA 90232

Chapter 15: Senator Ben Sasse
Sassy McSassy

5.24.18

Senator Ben Sasse
B40E Dirksen Senate Building
Washington DC 20510

Dear Senator Sasse,

Congratulations, you are letter #14 in my ongoing campaign to handwrite letters to each and every one of the Republican United States Senators.

It's my general understanding that you, Senator, are one of the good ones. Of course I use that term only in the most relative sense of the word.

What do I mean?

Let me use an example. We can all agree there are many crappy foods on the Taco Bell Fiesta Platter. All will induce painful stomach cramping as well as loose, runny bowel movements that may last for days.

But the Chalupa has a smattering of lettuce and tomato and protein-rich beans, containing some, not much, recognizable nutritional value. You sir, are the Chalupa on the US Senate Fiesta Platter of Incompetency and Corruption.

You may be asking, *"What have I done to deserve such derision?"*

MR. SIEGEL WRITES TO WASHINGTON

For that, let us turn to the pages of Exodus and the Hebrew's celebration of their passage, whereupon one son turns to his father before the ceremonial Passover meal and says,

"What makes this day different from any other?" (OK, he says night but that's not important)

Because on this day, your president, your Commander in Chief, the head of your political party has launched a scorched Earth attack on our Justice Department and the FBI. If I may borrow a phrase from the imbecile's vernacular: *The likes of which this world has never seen.*

He has undercut and undermined one of the cherished institutions that has served this nation and put in place the guardrails that keep our democracy on track.

And you, Sassy McSassy have said and done nothing.

NOTHING!!!

Even more appalling is the fact that you are a graduate of Harvard University. With a doctorate in History from Yale University.

You are a man of Letters and yet you choose to ignore your Senate responsibilities and enable this authoritarian to run roughshod over our Constitution.

You know better.

I know you know better.

Your constituents in Nebraska know better. Ok, maybe they don't. They're still trying to figure out how the expansion strap on the back of their MAGA cap works.

There can be only one explanation for your non-response.

You want to get re-elected. You want to get re-elected so badly that you are willing to ignore your duties, the oath you took and all manner of common decency just so you can go back to your cushy job in DC.

You are what we in the corporate world call a careerist. You've cravenly put your ambitions and political aspirations above all else. Moreover you've done it at a time when our nation desperately needs backbone and fortitude.

Today, my rage is running on the redline. Let me leave you with this:

Трахните тебя, Sasse.

I'm sure one of your aides, who might even be a FSB mole, can translate that for you.

Best,

Rich Siegel
siegelrich@mac.com
Culver City CA 90232

Chapter 16: Senator Orrin Hatch
Mr. Magoo

5.31.18

Senator Orrin Hatch
104 Hart Office Building
Washington, DC 20510

Dear Senator Hatch,

First let me say that in deference to your advanced age (84) I have decided to write this letter using large type. I didn't do that for any of the Republican US Senators I have been writing letters to and as recipient #15, I hope you will appreciate the gesture.

While researching your biography I found, much to my disappointment, that you plan to retire in January of 2019. It's my sincere hope that I can get you to rethink that decision and continue to represent the caffeine-free people of Utah.

Our country finds itself facing many dilemmas: corruption, campaign finance abuse, foreign intervention into our elections, and a blinding lack of moral clarity. Now, more than ever, we need energetic, fresh-thinking, 84 year old problem-solvers like you.

Stay Senator, stay.

Remember when our president had a hissy fit on live TV when he found out that law enforcement agents, with warrants in hand, raided the offices of Michael Cohen, and called our brave men and women in blue, *"stormtroopers"* and described the incident as *"an attack on our country."* You could not hobble over to a microphone fast enough to stand beside the people sworn to our safety and security. It was so inspiring.

Stay Senator, stay.

And there was Charlottesville. That's in Virginia, one of the original 13 colonies. A young woman lost her life there. She was mowed down by an alt. right Neo Nazi, one of the *"very fine people."* But you, Mr. Hatch, would have none of that. History will long remember your filibuster in the halls of Congress, wherein you demanded our President apologize for such a disgraceful characterization of this hideous murder. Your courageous stand will be written about in textbooks, discussed in classrooms and held up as shining example of steely leadership.

Stay Senator, stay.

Now, more than ever, we need a man with your incredible vigor, stamina and on-the-fly ability to tackle the tough challenges of the day. If you were to leave, where, oh where, would we find a similarly skilled, clear minded octogenarian who could steer us strongly into the 21st century? And beyond.

Stay Senator, stay.

I'll let you get back to Matlock now.

Best regards,

Rich Siegel
siegelrich@mac.com
Culver City, CA 90232

Chapter 17: Senator John Kennedy
The Conundrum

6.7.18

Senator John Kennedy
SR 383 Russell Senator Building
Washington, DC 20510

Dear Senator Kennedy,

You are an enigma. An enigma wrapped in a riddle and stuffed inside a Louisiana crawfish.

You have the Kennedy name, synonymous with the New England Dynasty of Democrats. And yet you identify yourself as a Republican and stand shoulder to shoulder with 50 other spineless creatures in the US Senate -- all of whom are receiving a personally hand written letter from yours truly.

This is letter #16. And I must say that in light of your momentary glimpses of sanity, you are perhaps the most puzzling.

When asked about the President's proposed military parade, you poo-pooed the idea, adding, *"confidence is silent and insecurity is loud."* Kudos.

When the scuffle arose about the President using the term shithole countries you paused and said, *"this is childish behavior. This is why aliens won't talk to us."* More kudos.

And who can forget -- thanks to the Internet and the viral video -- your grilling of a Precedent Shitgibbon nominee, Matthew Spencer Petersen, for a federal judgeship.

In that legendary 4:48 interview it became painfully obvious this shill of a candidate lacked the credentials for a lifetime appointment to the federal bench. In fact, he lacked the credentials and wherewithal to argue a traffic ticket in a municipal courthouse.

I suspect that had Jimmy Kimmel taken his cameras out on Hollywood Blvd. and conducted one of those embarrassing interviews where passersby cannot even identify the combatants of World War II, you'd still find a majority of people who better meet the criteria for that judicial position.

He was that bad. You brought it to light. Thank you. Here's a basket full of kudos.

You'd think that if the president, who regularly boasts of hiring the *best people*, nominates someone like Matthew Spencer Petersen, it would raise a red flag.

Did it not send a message to you?

Did it not make you wonder about the Precedent Shitgibbon's judgment?

Or his understanding of the gravitas of the position?

Compound that with this week's obvious lying about the letter he dictated in response to Don Jr.'s meeting with Russian intelligence officers.

Pile on the incomprehensible ramblings of the president's personal lawyer Rudy Giuliani, who speculated (out loud) about the possibility of assassinating former FBI Director James Comey. Let's not forget the time Captain Ouchie Foot fantasized about shooting a New Yorker on 5th Ave.

As if all that weren't enough, yesterday we had the president suggesting he could pardon himself, thereby placing himself squarely above the law.

I would think even paint chip eating Matthew Spencer Petersen knows that's a ridiculous legal contention.

Which brings us to the biggest mystery of all Senator Kennedy, why are you standing with this dim, frothy hugger mugger of a president and more importantly, why haven't you called for his impeachment?

Maybe it's time to stop sipping on those Bourbon Street Hurricanes and start refreshing yourself with a remedial reading of the US Constitution.

Best regards,

Rich Siegel
siegelrich@mac.com
Culver City, CA 90232

Chapter 18: Senator Mike Crapo
The Crapinator

6.13.18

Senator Mike Crapo
239 Dirksen Senate Building
Washington, DC 20510

Dear Senator Crapo,

Let's get to the good stuff first: your name.

One might contend that you are the most aptly named US Senator. I know all 51 because I am currently on a campaign to hand write letters to every Republican Senator for no other reason but to amuse myself and vent my DefCon Level One anger.

The truth is, Crappy, that honor goes to three of your colleagues, Senator GrASSley, Senator BarASSo, and Senator SASSe, all of whom demonstrate a level of ASShattery that befits their moniker. I mean come on; their names literally have ASS in it.

But let's not diminish the crappy job you have done representing the fine cattle ranchers, farmers and white supremacists in Idaho.

I took the liberty of looking over your Wiki page, because let's face it no one in America, with the exception of some ammo-sexual Neo-Nazis in Coeur d'Alene, knows who you are or what you've done.

Let's just say I was not disappointed in the least. When it comes to being a crappy person, you sir are more than worthy of the title.

And I'm not just referring to your 2012 arrest for drunk driving. Nor your encore Foster Brooks performance, when you got arrested for DUI again in 2013.

Mmmmm, vodka.

Which is odd considering you describe yourself as faithful member of the Church of Jesus Christ of Latter Day Saints. Drinking and driving doesn't seem so saintly to me.

If you were smart like our current EPA Secretary Scott Pruitt you would've had a special bulletproof limo built for your late night binging escapades.

I also see that you supported a bill that would make it illegal for a 17-year-old girl to cross state lines and get a legal abortion.

Funny, I was under the mistaken impression that Republicans were all about smaller government and less intrusion into our civil rights. How could I have gotten that so wrong?

What I find most impressive, Senator, is your "who gives a crap" attitude towards gun violence.

In 2012, when 20 families in Sandy Hook, Connecticut were busy burying their 6 and 7 year old children who were mowed down by an AR-15, you promised to filibuster any attempt by the Democrats to institute any sane gun control laws whatsoever.

Your empathy knows no bounds.

In 2017, you introduced the Hearing Protection Act. Making it easier for pistol aficionados to purchase and use gun silencers.

You're not just out there at the forefront to safeguard the rights of gun owners; you're manning the front lines to protect the hearing abilities of anybody who might find themselves within eardrum-busting gunshot range.

Let's face it, the "right" to listen to the jingoistic "music" of Toby Keith or Trace Adkins surely trumps the rights of sloppy kindergartners who might want to play with the Legos and do some figure painting in a safe school environment.

That's the type of forward thinking that is emblematic of today's GOP.

More importantly, it's just what one would expect from a guy named Crapo.

Have a nice day,

Rich Siegel
siegelrich@mac.com
Culver City, CA 90232

Chapter 19: Senator David Perdue
Commander Cavalier

6.19.18

Senator Perdue
455 Russell Office Building
Washington, DC 20510

Dear Senator Perdue,

You're a peach.

That's not a just a semi-clever reference to your standing as Georgia's junior senator, I mean you're a peach.

As in one of a kind.

A standout.

Unique in every sense of the word.

Let's be honest, you're not one of the handful of US Republican Senators who normally grabs a headline or gets any digital ink on the interwebs.

But yesterday, you changed all that. You bravely ventured into the dangerous waters of our current immigration crisis -- and yes, separating babies from their mothers merits the word crisis -- and you took a stand, albeit one that might be associated with a career minded colonel in the Third Reich.

MR. SIEGEL WRITES TO WASHINGTON

At a Senate Press Conference designed to address $15 billion in wasteful spending cuts, you said, *"This (the spending cuts) is the No. 1 topic in America today."*

Adding, that the situation at the border where young children were being pried away from their mothers by uncaring border patrol agents was simply, *"...the current shiny object of the day."*

Bravo, Senator, Bravo. Or shall I address you as Herr Gruppenfuhrer?

You have given the word cavalier new meaning.

This should come as no surprise. You literally have a Black Belt and a PhD in Cavalierness, stemming from your long storied business career.

Following your time at Georgia Tech, where you were a brother at the Delta Sigma Phi fraternity --a frat boy, how surprising --you also put in time at Sara Lee, Haggar Slacks, Reebok, and Pillowtex.

You remember Pillowtex don't you, Senator? You spent 9 months there.

Enough time to gestate a generous compensation package of $1.7 million for yourself. While simultaneously driving the company into the ground and pink slipping 7,650 workers. The closing resulted in the largest single-day job loss in the history of North Carolina.

Peachy.

With that kind of financial acumen, is it any wonder you found your way into the hallowed halls of Congress?

It goes a long way towards explaining your indifference to the suffering of these brown "people" at the border. I use quotations marks because I'm not certain that you see them as fellow human beings.

I can picture you and your wife and your two sons David Jr. (that's not cliché) and your other son Blake (nor is that) gathered round the huge 70 inch flat screen 4K TV in your palatial estate on Sea Island, downing a pitcher of mint juleps and watching the drama at our southern border unfold.

I have no problem imagining you, perhaps in a seersucker suit or at the very least proudly wearing a flag pin in the lapel of your navy blue blazer, sitting in your leather club chair and taking no small amount of glee in the plight of a screaming mother who just watched her 17 month old daughter being hauled off to a Tender Age Shelter.

And then in a mighty display of your trademarked insouciance, I can hear you topping your fellow warrior of the Reich, Corey Lewandowski, issuing the following response..."*Womp. Womp. Womp.*"

Have a nice day, Assclown.

Rich Siegel
siegelrich@mac.com
Culver City, CA 90232

Chapter 20: Senator James Inhofe
Colonel Snowball

6.27.18

Senator James Inhofe
205 Russell Senate Office Building
Washington, DC 20510-3603

Dear Senator Inhofe,

We're heading into the dog days of summer. Are you still making snowballs?

To be honest, I did a Google search and re-watched your escapade in the halls of Congress. I had to convince myself someone could actually be that stupid.

Holding up a snowball as evidence to debunk global warming is akin to holding up a rock and suggesting there is no intelligent life on Earth. Though, in your case, I'd be inclined to accept the premise.

Damn, you are one dull-witted son of a bitch.

I'm kicking myself in the pants for waiting this long to get to you. See, I've been writing letters to every Republican in the US Senate and surprisingly, your letter has been preceded by 18 others. Which gives you some idea as to the monumental cluelessness of your brown-nosing colleagues.

If I may indulge in some further transparency, I'm going to take it pretty easy on you Senator, even though the 20,000 regular readers of my blog love when I take the thrashing stick to one of you clods.

The reasons are twofold.

You simply haven't done much in your 20 plus year career in the Senate. Rubberstamping Precedent Shitgibbon's idiocy hardly counts as an achievement.

Secondly, and perhaps more importantly, I'm a little beat down today.

Watching our democracy circle the toilet bowl is quite draining. I'm sure it doesn't bother you to see our Supreme Court legitimize religious discrimination, but for someone with Hebraic roots, it hurts.

And I'm sure you're equally indifferent to the plight of Central American babies snatched from the arms of their asylum-seeking mothers. White privilege, like an American Express Black Card, is something I will never understand.

Besides Senator, when all is said and done, your legacy has been cemented in time. There is nothing I can say or write to add to it.

You are now, and will forever be, that schmuck with the handful of sooty DC snow.

A century from now when your great, great grandchildren are scouring our dystopian landscape looking for fresh water and maybe a few cockroaches to eat, they might stumble upon an old history book that somehow escaped the tsunami of seawater that arose from the melted ice caps.

MR. SIEGEL WRITES TO WASHINGTON

And in that algae-covered history book they will see how you bravely fought off the big bad Nobel Prize winning scientists and climatologists with their fancy data and dire global warming projection models.

Those great, great grandchildren, sporting tattered moldy clothing and matted hair, will read how, like David did to Goliath, you slew those elitist know-it-all geeky scientists, with your powerful, perfectly-formed snowball.

Nice work, Jimmy, nice work.

Best,

Rich Siegel
siegelrich@mac.com
Culver City, CA 90232

Chapter 21: Senator Steve Daines
Sir Verschränkung

7.11.18

Senator Steve Daines
1 Russell Senate Courtyard,
Washington, DC 20510

Dear Senator Daines,

Or shall I address you as Senator Schrödinger? As you seem to have mastered the time/space continuum and now have the ability to be in two places at the same time.

Last week, you pulled off this miracle of science, perhaps the biggest breakthrough in physics since the splitting of the atom. Or the invention of the Clapper.

There are pictures of you and your wife at a 4th of July fireworks celebration in Washington DC. There are also published pictures of you, alongside 7 other Republicans (*The Prostrate Eight*) at a conference table with your new Russian overlords in Moscow.

How can this be? Particularly since a cursory check of the airline schedule shows it to be physically and logistically impossible.

This can mean only one of two things, Senator.

Either you're a boldfaced liar, like the other 19 Republican Senators who I have already corresponded during my yearlong campaign of letter writing.

MR. SIEGEL WRITES TO WASHINGTON

Or, through the dint of hard work and good old fashioned American ingenuity, you and your lovely wife have broken through into the fifth dimension and now have the capacity to effortlessly defy the physical laws of nature that govern the rest of us mere mortals.

I have trouble believing the first choice -- that you're a liar -- particularly in light of what we now know of the high character and integrity of Montana people. Watching your constituents at Precedent Shitgibbon's rally last week was simply inspiring.

I could not believe my eyes when thousands of loving and caring Montanans walked out of that arena when the Commander in Chief began disrespecting and berating a national war hero like John McCain.

Watching them turn their back on our president when he started denigrating the charitable efforts of former President Bush choked me up as well.

It was so inspiring.

You must be so proud of those good folks from Bozeman, Billings and Butte. Those are exceptional Americans at their exceptional best.

And so, there can be only one conclusion, Senator Schrödinger.

You have transcended time, eluded space and accomplished what Einstein, Newton and Neils Bohr could only have dreamed of.

Even more impressive is that -- and yes I've taken the trouble of reading your online bio -- your formal schooling never went beyond a bachelor's degree at the highly prestigious Montana State University.

RICH SIEGEL

Color me impressed.

If I didn't have to wait for the electrician to show up to replace a blown fuse for the master bathroom, I would come all the way up to Montana just to shake your hand. Of course, with your newfound quantum leaping powers you could simply pop in to Culver City any time you'd like.

Please do Steve; I'll put on a pot of coffee.

Best,

Rich Siegel
siegelrich@mac.com
Culver City, CA 90232

Chapter 22: Senator Joni Ernst
Joni Loves Donnie

7.26.18

Senator Joni Ernst
825 B&C Hart Senate Office Bldg.
Washington DC 20510

Hi Joni,

Pardon the informality but after reading how much you used to like wrestling with the pigs and such, I didn't think you'd mind. In fact, I think you'd prefer that to the more stately "Dear Senator."

By the way, it should be noted that you are letter #21 in my yearlong campaign to correspond with each and every Republican Senator in our venerated upper house of Congress. I can't tell you how satisfying it has been to begin a real live dialogue with our US Senators.

No, literally I can't tell you.

Because to date, I haven't received one letter or email back. Nice to know our representatives value the opinions of the common man. Or, in my case, the foul-mouthed, bitterly cynical man.

I'm writing to you today because after a perfunctory look at some wiki pages, I noticed that your state, Iowa, is the second leading producer of soybeans.

In years past, most notably the Obama years, when there weren't any trade wars going on, this might have been a point of pride. But today, in the dysfunctional era of Precedent Shitgibbon, the mention of soybeans can only lead to heart palpitations.

Last I heard, the price on a bushel of soybeans had been cut in half. And with the tariffs, in China and in Europe escalating, those prices only have one way to go -- down.

Which means there'll be a glut in the market.

Which means you're likely to encounter some very pissed off farmers at your next town hall.

I've gotten way out in front of myself haven't I, Joni?

Because just yesterday, Captain Ouchie Foot announced a new $12 billion subsidy package to soybean farmers.

Hallelujah.

Now these farmers can jump on the government gravy train. They can start suckling on the teat of the American taxpayer. They can become the new welfare queens of the Midwest.

Our farmers, who once set the standard for hard work in America, can finally take a stroll down Easy Street.

If there's a check from Uncle Sam in the mailbox, why get up at 4 in the morning?

Why not sleep in? Wake and Bake. And cozy up on the couch to watch some Maury Povich and Wendy Williams.

MR. SIEGEL WRITES TO WASHINGTON

If I didn't know better, I'd say this smacks of socialism.

But I do know better, because according to the words of the wise man in the White House who said, *"What you're seeing and what you're reading isn't really happening."*

Right Joni?

Rich Siegel
siegelrich@mac.com
Culver City, CA 90232

Chapter 23: Senator James Lankford
Blanky Lanky

8.2.18

Senator James Lankford
316 Hart Senate Building
Washington, D.C. 20510

Dear Senator Lankford,

Recently, you were interviewed on ABC News and were asked about the Special Counsel's investigation into the Russian attack on our sovereignty.

You said, and I want to get this right, *"the whole thing has gotten confused because Americans turn on the TV everyday and regardless of what channel or where they go to look for news online or in print, it's constantly something else seems to be the story."*

Maybe that's Oklahoma-speak, but that's a lot to unpack.

But just as I have with the 21 letters to other Republican US Senators (part of my year long, letter writing effort) that have preceded this one, I'm game.

First of all Senator, people should not be getting their news from TV. Television is good for getting the latest sports scores, dishing on the Kardashians or even Jeopardy.

Do you have Jeopardy in Oklahoma, or do they just run Wheel of Fortune back to back?

MR. SIEGEL WRITES TO WASHINGTON

Secondly, and more importantly, why do you presume to speak for the American people? Maybe you and your constituents are confused, but I'm not.

For instance:

* I know collusion is a non-binding euphemism for conspiracy (a crime)

* I understand the notion of *Kompromat*, thus explaining the president's supplication. I already pre-ordered the Pee-Pee tape

* I see a team of Precedent Shitgibbon's campaign accomplices who had more than 120 illicit meetings with Russians prior to the election

* I recognize cover-ups, obfuscation and authoritarianism in plain sight (I wish the GOP did as well)

* I follow the comings and goings of Felix Sater, Victor Vekselberg, Deripashka, Boris Epstyn, Bayrock, Erik Prince, George Nader and many more.

It's deep.

It's robust.

It's slimy and it's un-American, but it's not confusing.

I can only surmise this has everything to do with what does or doesn't pass for intelligence in the great state of Oklahoma.

A storied keystone of our nation that has given us the Grapes of Wrath, corn as high as an elephant's eye, surreys with fringes on top and of course, the crown jewel contribution to western civilization, Brian Bosworth.

I'll be the first to admit that these are nothing but low, cheap shots based on hackneyed stereotypes and clichés. But that seems to be the coin of the realm these days, doesn't it Senator?

Not thanks to my president, Barack Obama, but thanks to yours -- Commander Half Brain.

If anyone is confused these days, I would suggest it's the GOP leadership.

In case you're drawing a blank, that's you, Senator.

Best,

Rich Siegel
siegelrich@mac.com
Culver City, CA 90232

Chapter 24: Senator Richard Shelby
The Commissar

8.9.18

Senator Richard Shelby
304 Russell Senate Bldg.
Washington, DC 20510

Dear Senator Shelby,

I have been around old people. I know that sometimes they say funny things. Or their minds have turned to mush.

"Grandpa, that's not the TV, that's the microwave oven. Come sit over here."

It is for that reason that I am willing to cut you, an 84 year old man, a little slack. For the record, if you've seen any of the 22 previous letters written to Republican US Senators as part of my yearlong campaign, you'd know that I'm not big on slack cutting.

Last month, you joined a group of fellow Republicans on a knuckle-headed trip to Moscow. And as part of the *Prostrate Eight*, you deferred, demurred and genuflected before your new Russian overlords.

And you did it all during the July 4th holiday, our national celebration of independence, freedom and liberty.

You have to admit, the optics on that suck.

RICH SIEGEL

Or, as they might say in the Motherland, *suckski*.

I have spent many years in the corporate business world and I know a little about reluctant supplication.

On many occasions, I answered to creative directors who were directors in no sense of the word, nor had any inkling of creativity.

For years, and for no other reason than to take home a biweekly paycheck, I bowed down to vice presidents and executive muckety-mucks who were nothing more than lumpish, tickle-brained clot poles.

And finally, and this one still sticks in my craw, at the peak of my career, I toiled silently -- ok, maybe not so silently -- for a drunken douchebiscuit who resided permanently at the bottom of a bottle of Smirnoff Vodka.

What I'm trying to say Senator is, *"I get it."*

At some point, at some time, for some reason, we all have to do what we don't want to do. So when Precedent Shitgibbon calls and says he needs you to do the Kremlin Two Step, you, a good ole boy from Alabama, put on your dancing shoes and board a plane to Gulagville.

But I'm scratching my hairless head over something else you did.

At the Helsinki Summit, Vlad the Dad suggested sending US diplomats and officials back to Russia to answer questions about crimes committed in the past. You know, for a friendly "interrogation."

To their credit, 98 US Senators, including every one of your Republican cronies, voted to deny sending anybody back for a Moscow Sit-down. Understandably, Senator John McCain, in the throes of brain cancer, did not participate in the vote.

MR. SIEGEL WRITES TO WASHINGTON

Un-understandably neither did you.

It's got me wondering.

How many rubles have they sent to your offshore bank account?

Were you promised a lavish dacha in Rublevka?

Is it Shelby or is it Shelboyevich?

Suddenly, that whole Crimson Tide thing makes a lot more sense.

Best,

Rich Siegel
siegelrich@mac.com
Culver City, CA 90232

Chapter 25: Senator Tim Scott
Stephen

8.23.18

Senator Tim Scott
717 Hart Senate Office Building
Washington, DC 20510

Dear Senator Scott,

I'm a white guy. You're not a white guy.

Race in America is a very tricky topic so I'm going to put on the kid gloves.

Who am I kidding? No, I'm not.

You see, although my skin is white, sometimes a bit more olive-like if I've been hiking or swimming with any regularity, I'm also MOT, a Member of The Tribe.

And in the eyes of many of your hooded South Carolina constituents, I, like you, are colloquially referred to as "mud peoples."

Isn't that nice?

Don't believe me, take a look at stormfront.com or vanguard.com or any of the thousands alt. right, all white websites who have spent the entirety of the 18 month Shitgibbon administration drooling over the prospect of Making America White Again.

MR. SIEGEL WRITES TO WASHINGTON

Hell, by now, the term mud peoples may have found its way onto the RNC website.

It pains me that I have to point this out to you. You seem to be blissfully unaware of your excessive melatonin.

Last year, for instance, you were nowhere to be seen or heard from when immediately after the incident at Charlottesville, Captain Ouchie Foot declared, *"there were very fine people on both sides."*

Really? Where were the very fine people on the Nazi side?

While one stormtrooper was plowing through the crowd in his Dodge Challenger were the "very fine people" off in a different part of town, refilling the tiki torches with fresh kerosene?

Did they stay back at the Comfort Inn to iron the khakis and polo shirts of their fellow fascists?

Maybe they were preparing snack trays and juice boxes? You know, kicking antifa ass and bullying the clergy at the local synagogue can really sap one's energy.

Face it Tim, you dropped the meat in the dirt.

And last week you picked up that year-old, filthy meat and decided to throw it on the grill and eat it.

After our fat, frothy flap dragon tweeted out some halfhearted pabulum -- *"I condemn all types of racism and acts of violence"* -- you demanded a soapbox so you could applaud his bravery and proudly proclaim...

"The President is showing signs of a better direction for the nation."

Good night nurse, are you playing the part of Stephen in Django Unchained II?

You're not convinced he's an out and out racist after the debacle with the Central Park Five, the housing discrimination suits, calling Africa a bunch of shithole countries, singling out NFL players, calling Omarosa a "dog", playing the low IQ trope, and literally standing at a press conference and saying out loud, "Where's my African American?"

You need to wake up and smell the *Strange Fruit*.

Get with the program, Tim.

Or is it Tom?

Best,

Rich Siegel
siegelrich@mac.com
Culver City, CA 90232

Chapter 26: Senator Roy Blunt
The Sultan of Unsubtlety

9.6.18

Senator Roy Blunt
260 Russell Senate Building
Washington, DC 20510

Dear Senator Blunt,

You Republican Senators make it so damn easy.

Allow me to explain.

Approximately 7 months ago I set out on a letter-writing mission to correspond with each and every Republican US Senator. With the exception of last week's posthumous letter to Senator McCain, in which I thanked him for upholding some standards of integrity, each missive has called attention to your collective and embarrassing dereliction of duties.

Upper house members, such as you, are responsible for acting as a check and balance on the Executive Branch. From what I can see, it's more like,

"Hey the balance in my savings account is low, I'll have Precedent Shitgibbon write me a check."

And oh how you aptly named senators have risen to the occasion. There's been Senator Crapo. And of course Senator Chuck GrASSley, Senator Ben SASSe, and Senator John BarASSo. I scoured the Wikipedia page hoping to discover Senator Douchebag. But before I could be disappointed, I ran across your name.

In that spirit Senator, let's get right to the fecal-throwing bluntness, if I may.

* You, and your 51 rim-licking colleagues, will go down in history as the most complicit congressmen and congresswomen to ever hold office.

* You, and your ilk, will be marked as collaborators. What Vichy was to the shame of France, you will be to the shame of our once great nation.

* You, and your cohorts, exhibit an unprecedented contempt for the Rule of Law and have no business being in a building that actually makes the law.

* You, and your cronies, have failed in every measure of moral leadership. Whether it comes to calling Nazis, *"very fine people."* Speaking up about hush payments to porn stars and Playboy bunnies. Remaining silent in the face of *"shithole countries."* Disgracing the honor of Senator McCain and his years of service and sacrifice. And turning the other way when, just a few days ago, the President of the United States chided the Department of Justice for daring to prosecute two Republican congressmen for corruption and fraud.

Allow me to be extra blunt, Senator.

You suck at your job.

MR. SIEGEL WRITES TO WASHINGTON

It kills me that my tax dollars put food on your table and provide healthcare for you and your worthless enabling family, including your three children, who not surprisingly grew up to be corporate lobbyists. That free healthcare should be going to people more deserving. And by that I mean any of the 8 billion other oxygen-breathing humans on the planet.

Perhaps I haven't been clear enough.

You, Senator Sycophant, with your phony grin and your Neanderthal views on reproductive rights, same sex marriage, "religious liberty" and easy access to assault weapons, are a rotting sack of maggot-infested camel shit.

Put as bluntly as humanly possible, the sooner the voters send you back to DonkeyButt, Missouri, the sooner we can start restoring this country to its former greatness.

Best regards,

Rich Siegel
siegelrich@mac.com
Culver City, CA 90232

77

Chapter 27: Senator Mike Lee
Inspector Insightful

9.13.18

Senator Mike Lee
361A Russell Senate Office Building
Washington, DC 20510

Dear Senator Mike Lee,

This country is full of naysayers.

Negative Nancies who have little faith in our government. People who are so upset with what they perceive as corruption, incompetence and outright douchebaggery in Washington, DC, they view politicians as lower than a NYC pizza rat.

I might have applied for membership in that club, but after seeing your rigorous interrogation of Supreme Court Nominee Bret Kavanaugh this week, my outlook on our future is decidedly more optimistic.

For the past 8 months, I've been writing letters to every GOP US Senator. You are letter #26. But if I can be quite frank with you, I had you inked for somewhere in the low 40's. That is, until I caught your Clarence Darrow-like performance on C-SPAN.

I'm no lawyer; I'm just a lowly advertising copywriter who delusionally sees himself tilting at windmills.

MR. SIEGEL WRITES TO WASHINGTON

And though I'm a little better versed in the law, thanks to the nightly tommyrot of the Constitution-shredding canker blossom in the White House, it should be noted I'm just a rank legal amateur. Nevertheless, I know *juris-brilliance* when I see it.

And since this letter is not only directed at you but will be published on my blog and eventually a book, I'll take the liberty of transcribing what can only be described as a seminal moment in our nation's history.

Because given the opportunity, and dare I say, the privilege of passing judgment on a candidate who will sit for a lifetime on the highest court of our land, taking his place beside judicial luminaries like Justice Marshall, Justice Frankfurter, and Justice Oliver Wendell Holmes, you went with this...

SENATOR LEE: I have a very important question for you.

KAVANAUGH hunches over in anticipation.

LEE: I notice that you take a lot of notes. And I respect that. Um...um...Because you're paying close attention. (DRAMATIC PAUSE) You use a Sharpie. And it's not a fine tip Sharpie. It's uh...regular Sharpie (making childlike circular motion) That might smudge and make a mess...why do you prefer that pen?

LEE: (drawing on his deep legal background) I'm just dying of curiosity.

KAVANAUGH: (stunned by the surgical precision of Lee's interrogatory skills) Uhhh.... so I can see it. It's nothing scientific.

AUDIENCE chuckles

LEE: That is a perfect mic-drop moment.

Ipso facto. QED. Sunset.

RICH SIEGEL

Take that Kamala Harris and Patrick Leahy and Cory Booker. That is how you conduct the people's business.

Forget all that Roe v. Wade nonsense. Or campaign finance reform. Or what constitutes an assault weapon and what is simply a gun with a high capacity magazine that can mow down 20 schoolchildren in less than a minute. The good folks of America want to get to the bottom of the writing utensil mystery.

Thank you Mikey. I don't know why people hold Harvard Law School in such high regard when it has become painfully clear, that your alma mater, Brigham Young, has produced our nation's finest legal scholars.

There can be no doubt this highly charged electric moment will find its way to the silver screen. Perhaps the next generation's Henry Fonda or Jimmy Stewart will bring your stellar insight to life in a performance that will live on for the ages.

Who knows, maybe this epochal snapshot in time is only a preview of greater things to come from Senator Mike Lee? Lee 2020?

Best,

Rich Siegel
siegelrich@mac.com
Culver City, CA 90232

Chapter 28: Senator Thom Tillis
Tar Heel Thom

9.20.18

Senator Thom Tillis
185 Dirksen Senate Office Building
Washington, DC 20510

Dear Senator Tillis,

I write letters. I write lots of letters.

About 8 months ago, I decided to write a letter to each and every one of the United States Republican Senators. You are number 26. Or 27. To be frank, I've lost track. There are so many of you pasty old white men and you seem to replicate like some alien life form possessed of inferior intelligence and offshore bank accounts.

To be even franker with you, I would have preferred to write a letter to Senator Cruz, because Ted has been in the news quite a bit this. You don't mind me calling him Ted, do you? It's a bit colloquial but it's also a lot easier than writing out bloviating, swag-bellied hedgepig.

Earlier this week, Ted, desperately fighting off an opponent who is clearly smarter, likeable and human, suggested that if he lost the election Texas would go ahead and ban BBQ. This is pure nonsense. As roasting strips of animal flesh over an open fire is to Texans as grabbing pussy is to Republicans.

But screwing the pooch once this week wasn't enough for Teddy (again, a lot easier than writing lumpish, sheep-biting maltworm.) He also made the mistake of suggesting that the nation had rushed to judgment with regards to the Dallas cop who entered the wrong apartment and shot an African American man dead.

For Christ's sake, the man was in his apartment, probably watching Sports Center and chewing on a week old Slim Jim and Johnny Po-Po comes bursting through the door. Fire, Ready, Aim.

Maybe Theodore (fewer letters than Twatwaffle) should spend less time watching porn and more time boning up on the law.

Clearly, he's no Senator Thom Tillis.

When word got out that Supreme Court nominee Bret Kavanaugh had racked up a whopping $200,000 in unpaid credit card debt -- because he enjoyed going to baseball games -- you put your foot down and did North Carolina proud, declaring the judge has *some esplainin' to do.*

When Senator Durbin provided documentation of Judge Kavanaugh's contradictory testimony regarding past involvement with waterboarding and other extreme interrogation methods, you rose up with mighty indignation rarely seen in the Dirksen Senate Building.

And when Professor Ford came forth and described in shocking detail how Bret Kavanaugh, a nominee to sit on the highest court in the land and shape our culture for the next 30-40 years, had attacked her and attempted to rape her, you made a beeline for the nearest microphone and camera...

MR. SIEGEL WRITES TO WASHINGTON

"This will not stand. This brave young woman has raised serious concerns. She has courageously come from behind the shadows and told us her harrowing story. Moreover, she has taken and passed a polygraph test. We have a duty to conduct a full scale FBI investigation. And, in the interest of serving our constituents, the American people, we must leave no stone unturned and put Judge Kavanaugh to the same rigorous standards and place him on the polygraph machine."

Oh wait, you didn't do any of that.

Turns out, Thom, you're more like Senator Cruz than I had assumed.

Just another frothy, beef-witted, barnacle-encrusted whey-face.

Best,

Rich Siegel
siegelrich@mac.com
Culver City, CA 90232

Chapter 29: Senator John Boozman
Boozman

9.27.18

Senator John Boozman
141 Hart Senate Office Building
Washington, DC 20510

Dear Senator Boozman,

Dude, is that your real name?

Or some holdover from when you were a DKE fraternity brother at the University of Arkansas? Frankly, I just can't get over how many United States Republican Senators have aptronyms.

APTRONYM
ˈaptrəˌnim/
noun --a person's name that is regarded as amusingly appropriate to their occupation

And believe me, I should know as I have made it my mission to hand write letters to each and every one of you buffoons and have already corresponded with Senator Crapo, Senator Blunt, Senator Ben SASSe, Senator GrASSley, and Senator Joe BarASSo.

Are you seeing the pattern here, John?

MR. SIEGEL WRITES TO WASHINGTON

Clearly, I could do Booze Man jokes until the drunken cows uber home.

"Hey Boozman, when you voted to kick elderly oncology patients off their affordable healthcare, were you on the floor of the Senate or did you phone it in from the Little Rock Tap N' Cap?"

Or,

"Hey Boozman, remember when that reporter asked you why you were in favor of tax cuts for the wealthy? And you replied, 'yeah, bring us some more topato skins. This time put some damn cheese and bacon bits in the topatoes."

I don't want to go down that expected path. I'm sure by this point in your life you've withstood every alcohol-soaked punch line in the book. Besides, you and I share something in common -- a love of rice.

Yours is obvious, because Arkansas is the country's largest producer of rice.

Mine, perhaps not so obvious.

Years ago I was brought in to work at an advertising agency on one of their biggest clients, Uncle Ben's Rice. I was given the opportunity to steep myself in the fascinating lore of rice. For close to two years I studied its history, its cultural impact and even its proper cooking technique. I even wrote a small booklet on *oryza glaberrima*

Oh, who am I kidding? Rice is nowhere near as funny as alky jokes.

Listen, Senator, today could be your day. A day to cement the Boozman name down in Congressional history.

RICH SIEGEL

What if, and I'm just spitballing here, you showed up at the Kavanaugh judicial hearings, waving a half bottle of Maker's Mark, left over from breakfast. And what if you interrupted Dr. Ford's testimony about sexual misconduct by shouting, *"Booooring."*

And then, in your best-drunk guy at a strip club voice you shouted *"Hey Grassley put on some music and bring out Candy with the big knockers. Come on Chuck, bring out Candyyyyyy!!!!"*

That would be epic.

You would no longer be that bland, slow-moving, slow-thinking guy from Arkansas with the big ears, you'd be a legend.

Don't let us down Boozman.

Rich Siegel
siegelrich@mac.com
Culver City, CA 90232

Chapter 30: Senator Cindy Hyde Smith
The Missing Miss of Mississippi

10.4.18

Senator Cindy Hyde Smith
113 Dirksen Senate Office Building
Washington, DC 20510

Dear Senator Hyde-Smith,

I am thoroughly confused.

Or as you might say in your home state of Mississippi, I don't know whether to check my ass or scratch my watch.

I'm as lost as last year's Easter Egg.

And as disoriented as a fart in a fan factory.

You see, for the last 9 months, I've been penning letters to all the US Republican Senators. Mostly to complain about the dim, frothy flap dragon that you and your colleagues call President.

Let's be honest Cindy, if brains were leather, that pussy-grabbing huggermugger wouldn't have enough to saddle a dust mite.

At this point in my mission, I thought I knew every senator on the list.

There are the Grade A Assclowns like Ted Cruz, Lindsey Graham and John Cornyn.

And then there are the walking dead cadavers from the 1800's, like Orrin Hatch, Chuck Grassley and Mitch McConnell. I'm sure each of these men has an embalmer on call 24/7.

And of course there are the semi-vertebrates like Bob Corker, Ben Sasse and Jeff Flake, who pretend to possess a moral compass but in all probability check the balances in their offshore bank accounts more often than a bloodhound licks his balls.

I bring this Senatorial checklist to your attention because it was only this morning that I discovered there were actually 4 female Republican Senators. Everyone knows Senator Lisa Murkowski and Senator Susan Collins, she of the ear-eating wobbly voice.

And even those of us who got past 10th grade are vaguely familiar with Senator Joni Ernst, who, when she's not shootin' AR-15's and Glock 9's, makes time to pass oppressive bills and spoon feed millions of dollars to our neediest billionaires.

But gaaaaawd damn, you'd have an easier time working up a legitimate *minion* of 10 Jews in Biloxi, Mississippi than finding a 'Merican who knew there were *four* female Republican Senators.

Senator, you put the hide in Hyde-Smith.

Maybe that's your shtick. You've got that invisibility thing down to an art. As a veteran of many large corporate organizations, I'm quite familiar with the tactic. Stay low, sit in the back at meetings, collect a check and quietly rise through the ranks by dint of attrition.

Last night you must have felt like queen of the prom.

MR. SIEGEL WRITES TO WASHINGTON

Because Captain Ouchie Foot flew all the way to Southaven, Mississippi, to stump for you. More accurately to stump for his Supreme Court nominee and Yale's most famous drunken boofer, Bret Kavanaugh.

And to accomplish that, he chose to stomp all over sexual assault victim, Dr. Christine Blasey Ford; in an attack that can only be described as vicious, heartless and brutal, perhaps even more brutal than the attack of 36 years ago.

And yet, you somehow managed to fly under the radar and protect your precious hide.

When pressed for a comment or a response to this decidedly Un-Christian blitzkrieg, your representative told reporters at the Picayune Item, *"Senator Hyde-Smith cannot be reached as she is flipping flapjacks for the Women's Auxiliary Group at the Abundance of Blessings Church in Kreole."*

Frankly, you are slicker than shit on a hoe handle.

Best,

Rich Siegel
siegelrich@mac.com
Culver City, CA 90232

Chapter 31: Senator Joe Manchin
The Manchinian Candidate

10.11.18

Senator Joe Manchin
306 Hart Senate Office Building
Washington D.C., 20510

Dear Senator Manchin,

This letter is as surprising to me as it is to you.

I'm fed up with the current Shitgibbon administration, but even more cheesed off with the lack of leadership from both Republican Chambers of the Congress. So nine months ago I decided to embark on a little homegrown project.

I would hand write a letter to every Republican US Senator.

Some, like the vapors-disabled Lindsey Graham and the Satanically-possessed Mitch McConnell, have merited two or three letters. By June of 2019, I should be completing my task. At which point all the letters will be published in a book, tentatively titled, "Mr. Siegel Writes to Washington" from Erupting Volcano Publications, Inc.

I never thought the book would also include a letter to a senior Democrat, but you changed all that when you put on your party dress and decided to dance with the devil and vote to appoint Bret "Tit and Clit" Kavanaugh to the Supreme Court.

I don't want to rehash the whole confirmation debacle. Replete with stories of ralphing, non-consensual groping, brewskis and rich white boy-entitled hijinks, it's a hangover best left in the past.

Besides, all of that doesn't make for intelligent political discourse between two grown men. And the 20,000 readers who will see this letter on my blog, roundseventeen.blogspot.com, expect more.

I prefer to take cheap shots at you and the great state of West Virginia, often referred to as the Switzerland of the Eastern Seaboard -- due to its landlocked nature -- and not because of anything nearing culture, or even civilization.

Let's start by saying I'm sure West Virginia, home of Cletus The Slack Jawed Yokel, couldn't be prouder of their US Senator. Just last year, West Virginia was ranked #47 (out of 50) in standard of living.

"Suck on that Arkansas, Oklahoma and Louisiana."

In terms of infrastructure, West Virginia came in dead last. Though I'm pretty sure if you polled West Virginians, that word might be a little confusing.

"Infrastructure? Sure, I got lots of stuff in my in-fro-structure, though we call it a shed, where I keeps my tools, my moonshine jugs and my girlie magazines that Brandy Lou don'ts let me keep in da house on account of the childrens."

Wow, you must be thinking.

Painting the entire state of West Virginia as a bunch of snaggle-tooth hillbillies happy to have a leaky roof over their heads, some minimal foot coverins' and a US Senator with no more intelligence than a half-eaten blueberry buttermilk scone ...that's a low blow.

But is it? Is it any lower than the President of the United States, standing before thousands of people, not to mention the national media, and openly mocking Dr. Ford, a woman who was the victim of a traumatizing sexual assault?

Is it any lower than a Supreme Court Justice who, when he wasn't demonstrating his partisan leanings and frat boy temperament, was lying about his proclivity for hurling and his participation in three way sword crossing?

Most pointedly, is it any lower than a Democratic US Senator, so eager to hold his precious seat of power that he sold out his constituents, and the future of the country, just so he can continue playing basketball in the Thursday Night Senate pick up games?

I don't think so.

Frankly Joe, I hope a camel with advanced pancreatitis shits in your cold cornpone.

Best,

Rich Siegel
siegelrich@mac.com
Culver City, CA 90232

Chapter 32: Senator Lisa Murkowski
Horseface

10.18.18

Senator Lisa Murkowski
522 Hart Senate Office Building
Washington DC, 20510

Dear Senator Horseface,

What's that? You don't like being called Horseface.

You find it debasing. Degrading.

And an insult to all women who deserve to be respected whether they bump fuzzies on film for our lascivious amusement or whether they occupy the lowest rung in our societal ladder and serve in the US Senate.

Yet, when your president took to Twitter yesterday to speak with his 41.7 million followers he took the opportunity to call a woman he was once intimate with, Horseface, with a capital H.

Amazing that the man your party elected to the same office held by Lincoln, FDR and George Washington, has once again demonstrated all the class of a second rate 1970's Times Square pimp.

Perhaps even more shameful, Senator Horseface, is the fact that neither you, nor any of your colleagues, stepped up and called out this brain dead pig and his boorish behavior.

I know because I checked your Twitter feed yesterday.

You had time to honor the Kenai Peninsula Ice Hole Fisherman of the Year, but not one word regarding the toxic misogyny oozing from 1600 Pennsylvania Ave.

You'd think that after writing 30 or so of these letters to Republican US Senators over the past 9 months, one of you would rise to the occasion. But you'd be wrong.

Frankly, I have more respect for the bukake gang bang girls who take spum baths for money than I have for any of you Congressional whores.

I'm a happily married man with two beautiful daughters and would never resort to calling a woman a Horseface. It's just wrong. Truth be told, I shouldn't have saddled that on you as well.

Besides, I looked at some no-so-flattering pictures of you on Google Images and honestly couldn't find any resemblance to a horse.

The buggy eyes and the thick helmet of hair however, do give you a certain goat-like appearance.

How about *Senator Lisa Goathead*?

Your halfhearted disapproval of Bret Kavanaugh notwithstanding, one could also argue your plodding, thoughtless behavior is distinctively ovine-like.

How about *Senator Lisa LambChop?*

Then again, perhaps I've been too hasty ruling out the entirety of the equine species.

MR. SIEGEL WRITES TO WASHINGTON

Because the fact that you remain a Republican and enable this morally bankrupt president who sanctions murders, who dirties the earth, who steals from the poor to give to the rich, who lies with every breath of oxygen he takes and who sucks on the titties of porn stars while his newborn son is suckling on his mother, tells me you are a Grade A Jack Ass.

Or, in deference to your gender, *Senator Jacqueline Ass.*

Best regards,

Rich Siegel
siegelrich@mac.com
Culver City, CA 90232

Chapter 33: Vice President Mike Pence
The Devil's Disciple

10.25.18

Vice President Mike Pence
The White House Office of the Vice President
1600 Pennsylvania Ave. N.W.
Washington, DC 20500

Dear Mike,

About 9 months ago, I embarked on a letter writing campaign. I compiled a list of the 51 United States Republicans Senators and week-by-week I pick one off and tell him, or her, exactly what I think of their cowardly, obsequious behavior, in terms that were anything but uncertain.

Technically, you are NOT a U.S. Senator.

But for reasons that still confound me, the authors of the Constitution mandated that you preside over the Senate in case there was ever a tie. Mind you, these are the same forward thinking clods and slave owners that said, *"The Negroes were only 3/5th human"*, *"women can't vote" and "citizens should have unencumbered access to military grade weapons."* So there's that.

I chose you this week for a special reason. And it has little to do with your party or your politics. And more to do with your piety, or lack thereof.

MR. SIEGEL WRITES TO WASHINGTON

You will recall that at the 2016 Republican National Convention you took to the podium and proudly announced that you, *"...come before the American people as a Christian, an American and as a Republican. In that specific order."*

You remember saying that, don't you Brother Mike? Of course you do, because your by-the-book Christianity is part and parcel of who you are. It's why Mother won't let you dine with another woman. It's why you view homosexuality as an abomination. And it's why you don't eat cheeseburgers or visit Red Lobster. Right?

Let's not forget that in addition to laying down with another man, mixing milk with meat and eating shellfish were all explicitly forbidden in the same passages from Leviticus.

But this week Mike was so goddamned special. Oooops.

Because this week we saw the Mac Daddy of all sins, MURDER, played out on the international stage. An American resident, a columnist for the Washington Post, and father of four American children, Jamal Khashoggi was butchered at the hands of the Saudi Secret Service.

I'd have to whip out the Charlton Heston DVD and skip past all that plague crap and that good stuff when God torches some bushes and splits the Red Sea with the breath in his nostrils, but I'm pretty sure if you look at those two stone tablets, the prohibition of Murder is right up there near the top.

Granted, Jamal Khashoggi's skin was a few shades darker than white. Ironically, closer in complexion to that of Jesus than anyone in the Hoosier State, but still an innocent, olive-skinned man lost his life for nothing more than speaking his mind and fighting for freedom of his people.

97

Yet, in light of all this, your boss, Captain Ouchie Foot, is willing to absolve the Saudis of a murder most foul, because of an arms deal that will pump 17 trillion million gazillion dollars into our economy and provide jobs and a Lamborghini for every man, woman and child in the Western Hemisphere -- his words, not mine.

And you're going to look the other way. Just as you looked the other way when he committed:

* Gluttony *("Give me two buckets of KFC tonight, that rally made me hungry.")*

* Adultery *("it's not really cheating, she had a Horseface.")*

* Pride *("I'm a stable genius.")*

* Bearing False Witness *(See 1946-2018)*

Let me lay this on you, Mike. I may be some atheist, hedonistic, alcohol-loving, fire-spitting Jew, but the truth is, I'm more Christian than you'll ever be.

In fact, if I get to Hell before you do, I'll save a seat and a frosty, minty mojito for you.

Best,

Rich Siegel
siegelrich@mac.com
Culver City, CA 90232

Chapter 34: Senator Pat Toomey
The Mortician

11.1.18

Senator Pat Toomey
248 Russell Senate Building
Washington, D.C. 20510

Dear Senator Toomey,

Happy Day After Halloween.

Hope your holiday was filled with pumpkin pie and little chocolate candies. Though I suspect, in light of the coldblooded mass murder of 11 Jews, inside a temple no less, your Halloween was filled with ghouls, ghosts and many visits to the bathroom to wash the blood off your hands.

Oh yeah, Senator, there can be no doubt you are an unindicted co-conspirator in this latest bloody pogrom.

I'm currently in the smack dab middle of my yearlong letter writing campaign to each of the Republican US Senators. I don't think I've ever been so eager to unload on one of you soulless, worthless, pasty white face assnuggets.

You see Pat, you watched this hateful tragedy unfold and then had the temerity to remain silent.

RICH SIEGEL

Sure, there were the empty tweets about "thoughts and prayers" and
"standing in unity with our Jewish brothers and sisters" -- you know
the boilerplate Hallmark crap -- but not a peep, not a goddamn word
about the Soros fear-mongering, the caravan conflation, the good
and noble work of the HIAS or the tribal scapegoating spearheaded
by your Commander in Chief, Precedent Shitgibbon.

NOTHING.

I would imagine your conscience is bothering you. But then I took a
look at your online bio and came to the conclusion that you don't
have one.

I suppose I should tip my hat to you.

You had all the makings of a moderately successful Assistant
Manager at a Pathmark. I mean if they were handing out trophies for
Mediocrity you'd be standing next to a shoulder-high, gold plated
beauty that would require its own particleboard cabinet. They would
have retired your blue polyester vest and immortalized your name at
the Pathmark Headquarters in nearby Iselin, New Jersey.

But no sir, you leveraged your marginal intellectual abilities, your
khaki-pants blandness, your toothy grin, and your Allegheny-sized
forehead into a position of power.

Moreover, unlike Senators Flake or Sasse who lamely attempt to
exhibit some moral backbone, you've wisely decided to choose the
better-paved path of rubberstamping each and every despicable act
of Captain Ouchie Foot.

Senator, you've elevated sycophancy to a high art.

MR. SIEGEL WRITES TO WASHINGTON

It takes a special kind of man to carefully align his political positions in perfect lockstep with an erratic, ill-informed, narcissistic, constitutionally-ignorant, bloated, swag-bellied hedge pig, but you were more than up to the task.

You managed to knock millions of people off healthcare. Give more than a trillion dollars to the super wealthy instead of rebuilding our nation's infrastructure. Stood up against gay people who had the audacity to demand equal rights. And took enough NRA money to earn membership in their Golden Crosshairs Club.

And as far as this latest incident...so what if 11 old Jews had to bite the dust, right? "Blood and Soil", isn't that the new catchphrase of the GOP?

My people like to say, may their memories be a blessing.

But for you, may their memories haunt you the rest of your days.

Best,

Rich Siegel
siegelrich@mac.com
Culver City, CA 90232

Chapter 35: Senator Rick Scott
Tricky Ricky

11.8.18

Senator Rick Scott
716 Senate Hart Office Building
Washington, DC 20510

Dear Senator Scott,

Welcome. Or shall I say Congratulations.

Because you have not only won a seat in the US Senate you've earned a spot in my upcoming book -- tentatively titled *Mr. Siegel Writes to Washington.*

You see I've made it my goal to hand write letters to all the US Republican Senators, none of whom are distinct and all of whom strike me as white privileged douchewaffles.

And now you're one of them.

To be more specific, you are letter #33.

But don't let that number fool you. I have plenty of fire and brimstone in me. And so rest assured, you, a newcomer to this prestigious club, will receive the same colorful, pungent and humiliating dressing down as some of your more luminous colleagues like soulless Mitch McConnell or spineless Jeff Flake.

MR. SIEGEL WRITES TO WASHINGTON

Believe me, it's not hard to build up a head of steam, particularly in your case considering your clay-brained, unchin-snouted approach to gun legislation.

Following the tragic shooting in Parkland, Florida (where you were governor) that saw teenagers mass murdered on their way to Math or English class, you moseyed on up to the NRA donation trough and begged for more money by endorsing Precedent Shitgibbon's call for armed teachers.

In other words, according to you, the solution to our nation's gun problem is more guns. What kind of twisted backasswards logic is that?

When Russian Politburo officials did a post-mortem on the catastrophe at Chernobyl, did they turn to each other and say, *"You know what would fix the core meltdown at this poorly designed and poorly engineered nuclear plant? More poorly designed and poorly engineered nuclear plants."*

And when Nazi Party members took inventory of the Hindenburg, I'm pretty sure those smart Germans didn't turn to each other and say, *"You know what our hydrogen-filled Zeppelins need? Candelabras."*

Seriously, what is it with you bald-pated hornbeasts?

I can only surmise that while other babies were being breast fed you were being raised on a steady diet of turpentine and DDT.

Or, that instead of cleaning your ears out with a Q-tip, your parents opted for the needle nose pliers.

Or, that while some students were preparing for their college SATs, you were still trying to navigate the opening questions on the MCAT, the Montreal Cognitive Assessment Test.

I don't know where all this dain bramage comes from. I only know that now that you're in the US Senate, you're going to fit right in.

Welcome home, Rick.

Best regards,

Rich Siegel
siegelrich@mac.com
Culver City, CA 90232

Chapter 36: Senator Lamar Alexander
Alexander the Not So Great

11.15.18

Senator Lamar Alexander
455 Dirksen Senate Office Building
Washington, DC 20510

Dear Senator Alexander,

Ten months ago I embarked on a writing journey. I set out to pen a letter to each of the United States Republican Senators. It's not an easy task as each week I am forced to go back over the list and take inventory, just so I don't duplicate my efforts.

To be frank, I thought I had written to you, as you have a very recognizable name.

To be even more frank, I thought you were dead.

I'm only 44 years old but I seem to remember hearing about you when I was kid.
Weren't you around for the Teapot Dome Scandal?

The other thing I've noticed about this continuing effort is that each week there is a fresh new scandal plaguing the Shitgibbon White House. This past week was unusual in that there were multiple debacles.

RICH SIEGEL

You had:

* The Big Blue Wave

* The Jim Acosta First Amendment Affair

* The disgusting response to California wildfires (more than 50 dead)

* The refusal to attend a World War I Memorial Service in France

* And the indefensible snubbing of our soldiers by not visiting Arlington Cemetery on Veterans Day. On VETERAN'S DAY!!!

I use the word indefensible because it appears that way to us.

But, apparently that collective "us" does not include members of the GOP. And least of all, Senators of the Republican stripe. Because to a man, woman and shameless bootlicker, you have all remained silent.

You'd think by now, two years into Captain Ouchie Foot's shabby administration these staggering indiscretions would just roll off my back like the warm vodka-infused urine coming from a Russian hooker.

But the truth is, these things make my blood boil.

Perhaps, as the senior senator from the great state of Tennessee, you've got other things on your mind and deserve special dispensation.

I have a friend who attended Cocke County High School. He's a proud Cocke and a Volunteer through and through. And he is always sending me news clippings from the Newport Plain Talk, a throwaway rag that seems to specialize in the colorful local tomfooleries that make Tennessee, Tennessee.

MR. SIEGEL WRITES TO WASHINGTON

From what I can tell, it can't be easy governing a state where Moonshining is a course requirement for every high school graduate.

Or where goats must be fitted for chastity belts.

Or where the tailpipe of every parked car is vulnerable to a midnight defiling.

I get it.

It's Tennessee and you've got your hands full, Senator.

Or as my friend Greg puts it, *"Tennessee, now with 37% more Florida."*

Best,

Rich Siegel
siegelrich@mac.com
Culver City, CA 90232

Chapter 37: Senator Roger Wicker
Rodger the Integrity Dodger

11.29.18

Senator Roger Wicker
555 Dirksen Senate Office Building
Washington, DC 20510

Dear Senator Wicker,

It certainly makes sense that I write to you today, as the great, prestigious and scholarly state of Mississippi, Home of the Hemp Necktie, is currently in the news.

Naturally this letter should be going to newly elected Grand Wizardress Cindy Hyde Smith, however she has already been crossed off the list of my yearlong letter writing campaign to all the US Republican Senators.

And so Senator your number is up. And what a fortuitous number, it is.

After my morning Old Fashioned, I took the liberty of using The Google and to read up on your lifetime of career achievements. If I might say so, finding you was like hitting the Mega Millions Super Powerball of GOP Ineptitude.

You are the quintessential Republican Senator and check off every box of Senatorial Unsuitability.

And then some.

MR. SIEGEL WRITES TO WASHINGTON

Let's go back to 2015 when you, a man of no scientific standing whatsoever, were the only Senator to vote against an amendment declaring climate change is real. I mention this because just this week, a staff of credentialed White House scientists found otherwise.

I can only assume that, like Precedent Shitgibbon, you are one of those people blessed with superior intelligence and despite the hard data, simply don't believe in global warming.

I'm also going to give you the benefit of the doubt and suggest your stand had nothing to do with the vast amounts of money you have accepted from the Oil and Gas Industry. Nor the unlimited guest account they have set up for you at Butchie's Beef & Reef Roadhouse on Route 39, just outside of Tupelo.
"Can I get more melted butter? And a new bib? I don't want to get any lobster juice on my new khakis."

Your hillbilly perspective on climate change is just the tip of the Ignorant Iceberg.

Who can forget that time you asked the Navy to prohibit a secular humanist to serve in the Chaplain Corps and administer to soldiers who might not share your beliefs in a Magic Sky Daddy?

Adding, *"It is troubling that the Navy could allow a self-avowed atheist to serve in the Chaplain Corps."*

I hate to trouble you even more, Roger, but you have a full-fledged atheist, a money grubbing, Commandments-defying atheist at that, currently living at 1600 Pennsylvania Ave.

You don't believe Captain Ouchie Foot is a real Christian, do you? If you're going to buy that jackassery about his favorite book, Two Corinthians, then I'd like to sell you 3BR, 2BA townhome in Boca Raton that just needs *a little tender loving care.*

Also, because I can see from your bio how devout you are, how exactly do you square your silence with your president separating kids from their mothers, locking them in cages, lobbing tear gas at women and children as well as actively aiding and abetting the cover up of a premeditated murder by the Saudi Prince?

Finally, since you were in the Air Force for 27 years, I'd love to know how you bit your tongue and stayed below the radar when Commander Jizztrumpet attacked Admiral McRayven, the man in charge of the Bin Laden takedown, and accused him of being some kind of Democratic political operative.

If attacking a decorated soldier like Admiral McRayven wasn't wrong enough, wouldn't you at least agree the President of the United States ought to have laid a wreath at Arlington Cemetery on Veteran's Day!

How abnormal is the current state of affairs? Ask yourself what the consequences be if our previous president -- the smart black guy -- had done the same thing? You're from Mississippi, I think you'd agree it would not be very pretty.

Best,

Rich Siegel
siegelrich@mac.com
Culver City, CA 90232

Chapter 38: Senator John Thune
A Tall Drink of Nothing

12.6.18

Senator John Thune
Dirksen Senate Office Bldg. #511
Washington, DC 20510

Dear Senator Thune,

Let me start by saying Mazel Tov.

It's my understanding that you have just been elected the new Senate Majority Whip, the second highest ranking among Republican Senators. You're replacing Senator Cornyn from Texas and you've wasted no time filling his shoes, finding the nearest microphone and immediately starting with the GOP Batshit Crazy.

Good on you, Senator.

And while we're at it, good for all your colleagues for their week in/week out nonstop parade of hubris and IBS-inducing Trump apologia. Just as a little background, I've made it my mission to hand write letters to all 53 of you Cro-Magnon bastards.

We're actually getting towards the end of the list, a position not unfamiliar to every South Dakotan. And for that matter, your equally forgettable neighbors to the North.

I did a little research and discovered that Sioux Falls, the largest city in South Dakota has a population of 185,000. Is that all?

On any given Friday night, there are 190,000 people waiting to get a table at Tsujita Ramen on Sawtelle Blvd. If you go there Senator, don't bother with the Miso broth, go with the pork belly.

I don't want to spend my time taking cheap shots at the Mount Rushmore state.

I'd rather concentrate on the rock-headed interview you gave last week when it was divulged, by Michael Cohen, one of the president's legendary "Best People", that our Great Muckle Gype had been in active negotiations with Vladimir Putin while running for President of these United States.

Let that sink into the sedimentary grey matter lodged between your ears, Thuney.
Because to those of us with a functioning brain stem, it says he's been lying all along. Ok, that goes without saying. But in this case, he's been hyper-lying. How many times has he stood in front of a microphone or sat on the porcelain throne and under the haze of too many Diet Cokes, tweeted, "No Collusion"?

He was colluding.

Not just with Russian oligarchs or made men from the Russian Mafia, but with VTB (a sanctioned Russian bank no less) with direct ties to the Kremlin.

I'm not sure they teach geo-politics at North Bunghole University, where you got your Masters in Wheat and Plainscaping, but Russia is our adversary. Has been for close to a hundred years. And they have this force of cutthroat spies, now known as the FSB but formerly known as the KGB. In 1998, little Vladimir Putin was put in charge of Russian Intelligence.

In short, he's an evil mastermind. To be even shorter, you'd have to be raised on airplane glue, or a lunkhead from South Dakota, to believe Putin gave a rat's ass about some shoddy-built fleabag hotel sporting the Trump name high atop the Moscow skyline. Putin did it to get his hooks into our own Precedent Shitgibbon.

Kompromat, Senator. *Kompromat*.

And yet, with these mind blowing revelations, on top of the growing mountain of evidence compiled by Mueller, a true patriot, you hunted down a reporter from Newsmax and said...

"I don't think that there has been anything that changes the landscape so to speak where the president is concerned."

As if that buffoonish jackassery weren't enough, you added that, *"it was time to draw this Mueller investigation to a close."*

A close, Senator? No. There are many, many, many questions that have yet to be answered. Not the least of which is: Where do they find clueless clods like you?

Also, when you ran track in high school, did you ever find yourself on the errant receiving end of a shot put?

Best regards,

Rich Siegel
siegelrich@mac.com
Culver City, CA 90232

Chapter 39: Senator Jerry Moran
Rock, Chalk, Jerry Moran

12.13.18

Senator Jerry Moran
Dirksen Senate Office Bldg. #521
Washington, DC 20510

Dear Senator Moran,

Can you smell it Senator?

I can smell it. 57% of Americans can smell it. It's the sweet, fragrant aroma of impeachment.

Last week, your president, Hogbellied Gudgeon #1, was named in a federal sentencing memo as an unindicted co-conspirator in the commission of criminal violations of Federal Election Campaign Laws.

That's not just a mouthful. That's a mind full.

Think about it Jerry, the ill-tempered, ill-informed imbecile sitting at 1600 Pennsylvania Ave., the schmuck who could, with the flick of an undersized stubby finger, blow the planet to smithereens, is a criminal.

While you ponder that, let me explain that I've been writing letters to all 53 of the US GOP Senators. You're number 36 or 37, to be honest, I've lost count. Sorry.

MR. SIEGEL WRITES TO WASHINGTON

But this letter is special. Why? Well, for one thing, sometime in the near future this letter will be published, with all the others, in a book. And as a service to my readers I feel the need to mix things up.

So today, unlike previous letters to your colleagues, I'm not going to harangue you about all the shitty policies you've endorsed and or the fascist, hypocritical legislation you've supported.

You see this letter is not about what you've done. It's about what you will no doubt do.

What makes me so prescient? Well, Senator, not only are you exceedingly vanilla and excruciatingly uninspired, you are also painfully predictable.
Therefore, to know how you will proceed with the upcoming impeachment trial for Captain Ouchie Foot, we need only to see how you voted in the impeachment hearing for a previous president, Bill Clinton.

And here's where it gets so interesting.

While you were a member of the House, representing the great state of Kansas, you unsurprisingly voted with the Republican majority to impeach President Clinton for lying about his extracurricular activities with Monica Lewinsky.

Not only were you quick to whip out the impeachment bomb, you felt the need to pile on and do a little grandstanding, telling a reporter from the Washington Post...

"Having to make a choice, I choose to be on the side that says no person is above the law; that this is a nation of laws, not men; that telling the truth matters; and that we should expect our public officials to conduct themselves in compliance with the highest ethical standards."

Lordy, if that could all fit on T-shirt, I'd commit those beautiful, articulate, inspirational words to Hanes 100% cotton.

If I were to understand that correctly, I assume you would apply those same *"high ethical standards"*, when it comes to time to judge He-Who-Consumes-No-Information-But-Buckets-of-Crispy-Kentucky-Fried-Chicken.

Because, let's be honest, banging a porn star and then doling out $130,000 (a week before the election) to hush the "horsefaced" one (his words, not mine) is certainly not kosher. Nor is money laundering, obstruction of justice or conspiring with Russkis to steal an American election.

Therefore it goes without saying and it's a simple slam-dunk that you will vote FOR impeaching the 45th President of the United States of America. Right? Because you said, *"no man is above the law"* and that *"telling the truth matters."*

You said that. But who are we kidding, Jerry? We both know, we all know, you're NOT going to do the right thing and vote for impeachment. You're simply not. I'd bet one of my two semi-functioning testicles on it. And here's why I'm so confident.

Like all Republican senators, your unwavering, unfathomable, and patriotism-free predictability is surpassed only by your equally reflexive hypocrisy.

Best,

Rich Siegel
siegelrich@mac.com
Culver City, CA 90232

Chapter 40: Senator Bill Cassidy
Doctor Doodie

12.20.2018

Senator Bill Cassidy
520 Hart Senate Office Building
Washington, DC 20510

Dear Senator Cassidy,

Bless you Senator. Finding you was like hitting the Etymological Jackpot.

Allow me to explain. Several months ago I set out on a mission to write letters to each of the Republican US Senators. While going about my self-appointed business, I noticed a weird phenomenon. You see many of your colleagues sport illustrative names that are apropos to what a Republican Senator in 2018 should be.

For instance, there's Senator Crapo.

For another instance, there's Senator Boozman.

Let's not forget Senator Blunt.

Nor Senator Flake.

Last week I wrote to Senator Moran, though it was mighty tempting to go with something more pejorative.

You see where this is going right, Bill?

Most intriguing however was the number of Republican Senators who lived up to their name in the most fitting way possible:

Senator GrASSley

Senator BarASSo

Senator SASSe

That's the holy trifecta of ASShattery.

Or so I thought. Because then I stumbled upon you. And judging from your distinguished record of non-achievement, I suspect stumbling is how most people find you.

But in ways too many count, I am so happy that you, Senator CASSidy were the ass-adjacent senator I found last. Sort of like saving that best piece of chocolate-frosted cake for the end.

I took the liberty of running down your bio on Wikipedia. You can just imagine my delight when I read about your "work" in the great state of Louisiana. And that before you were in public service, you were in the service of private parts. More specifically, you were an accredited gastroenterologist.

You were literally in the Ass Business.

Or is it the Business of Ass?

You put food on your table by making sure the food of other people did not get stuck in their Alimentary Canal.

That takes the cake.

MR. SIEGEL WRITES TO WASHINGTON

Between the daily ass backwards antics of Precedent Asshat and the ass-kissing by you and your asinine Vichy-enabling associates, you have all secured quite a special place in the annals of history.

I'll leave it right there, Senator, as I feel a sudden urge to wash my hands.

Best,

Rich Siegel
siegelrich@mac.com
Culver City, CA 90232

Chapter 41: Senator Richard Burr
The Admiral

12.27.2018

Senator Richard Burr
Russell Senate Office Building,
217 Constitution Ave NE,
Washington, DC 20510

Dear Senator Burr,

Or do you prefer Richard Burr?

Or the more colloquial, Dick Burr?

Senator, I don't know if you've noticed this, but you and many of your colleagues, Boozman, Crapo and Blunt, have some strange, surreally appropriate surnames.

I know this because I have been writing letters to each and every Republican US Senator as part of a my own personal mission. It goes without saying that I have taken great joy pointing out the foibles and failures of the upper house.

I've said this before, but it's like shooting fish in a barrel.

Flat fish, like flounder or halibut. Flat dead fish that don't move or show any signs of brain function.

MR. SIEGEL WRITES TO WASHINGTON

You walk those underground tunnels and maybe even share a chicken salad sandwich with these folks at the congressional commissary, you know exactly what I'm talking about.

If I may...

"They're criminals. They're drug money takers. And they're racists, though some, I assume, are fine people."

But I'm going to go easy on you, Dick.

For one thing, it's only a couple of days past Christmas. And though I don't officially celebrate the holiday, I do enjoy the downtime and the opportunity to indulge in some day drinking. Particularly when there's a bottle of Noah's Mill bourbon within sleeve distance.

The other reason, and this one is such an anomaly that it has quite frankly thrown me for a loop, is that you've actually done something right.

By most accounts, you and your Democratic partner Senator Warner have run a truly bipartisan Senate Intelligence Committee.

In these contentious times, that's quite admirable.

I'm sure Congressman Devin Nunes, your house counterpart, is a tad jealous of your functional bipartisanship. Actually, I don't think that clueless soap dish of a man can even spell bipartisan.

Just last week you did what heretofore seemed impossible from someone of your stripe. You put country before party and submitted to the Special Counsel's office a list of witnesses you now suspect lied before your committee.

Hit me in the face with a hot waffle iron.

I never thought I'd see the day.

In light of all that, I'm going to leave this letter on a pleasant note and wish you a Happy New Year.

I'm also giving fair warning to next week's recipient. There's a good chance I'm going to go off on him, or her, with all the fury of a defective Russian-made pressure cooker.

Best,

Rich Siegel
siegelrich@mac.com
Culver City, CA 90232

Chapter 42: Senator Shelley Moore Capito
The Pride of Appalachia

1.3.19

Senator Shelley Moore Capito
117 Russell Senate Office Building
Washington, DC 20510

Dear Senator Capito,

Last week, my surging Syracuse Orange football team put a beat down on your West Virginia Mountaineers at the 2018 Camping World Bowl.

I believe the score was 138-0.

I might have the exact score wrong. But as a senator working with the Trump administration I'm sure you've come to realize the futility and unimportance of specific numbers. The same goes for words, facts and truths. They're all fair game and up for subjective interpretation.

Nevertheless, when it came to time to award the prestigious Camping World trophy, they handed it to my team. Not yours. Your team was already in the locker room munching on ginseng roots and drowning their sorrows in rotgut moonshine.

And so when it came time to pen this week's letter to a Republican US Senator, part of my mission to write to each and every one of you sycophantic overachievers, I knew I had to seek out the representative from the Kissing Cousin State.

You can imagine my surprise when I discovered that the legendarily progressive people of West Virginia had sent a member of the fair haired sex to represent them in Washington DC.

My lord.
What's next?
Are they gonna allow womenfolk to drive automobiles?

For readers who will be seeing this letter in a forthcoming book, it should be noted that you, Shelley, have only been in the US Senate since 2015. So it would be unfair to lump you in with the Hatchs, McConnells and Grahams of this world, who have spent decades in the Upper House, accomplishing so little.

Though they have successfully penned their legacy to future face palming historians who will look back at this administration and think, *"WTF?"*

Besides Shelley, you, a dyed-in-the-wool Republican and a former Cherry Blossom Princess, and me, a half Jew, half Scottish wise ass from the Bronx, NY, have something very unique in common. Both our fathers are convicted criminals and have spent considerable time in prison.

How weird is that?

My father was caught smoking marijuana in 1947 while serving in the US Army. They arrested him, court martialed his butt and threw him in jail for a year at Camp Gordon in Georgia.

Your father pleaded guilty to five felonies including extortion and taking more than 1/2 million dollars in illegal payments from the Maben Energy Corporation. He spent close to three disgraceful years in a cushy federal prison. And another few months in supervised home confinement.

MR. SIEGEL WRITES TO WASHINGTON

But here's the thing, Shell.

Marijuana is now legally sold in many states and so my father's youthful indiscretions would barely register a glance from authorities.

Your daddy, however, would still be in the clink. As corruption, illegal campaign contributions, extortion and lying under oath are still felonies. Well, at least as of this writing they are.

Before this is over, the Bumbling Bawbag in the White House may request that you and your cronies rewrite the laws to change all that.

And if past is prologue, naturally you will oblige.

Best,

Rich Siegel
siegelrich@mac.com
Culver City, CA 90232

Chapter 43: Senator Pat Roberts
The Sardar of Sarcasm

1.10.19

Senator Pat Roberts
109 Hart Senate Office building
Washington, DC 20510

Dear Senator Roberts,

News broke last week that you will not be seeking reelection to represent Kansas in 2020. That's sad.

The good news is you'll be around long enough to be included in my book of letters to every Republican US Senator. In fact, you are letter #41.

It's hard to believe an energetic and youthful 82-year-old man like you would give up his powerful seat in the Senate. Frankly, I don't know how they will continue on without you.

I'm sure the good folks in Topeka are planning to honor you for your legendary service. But in case they get sidetracked by a tractor pull or another red golf cap rally to genuflect at the feet of our Massive Orange Bellend, let me take this opportunity to go through some of the career highlights of Senator Pat Roberts.

Let's start with the issue you and many of your colleagues believe is a non-starter.

MR. SIEGEL WRITES TO WASHINGTON

You famously said, *"There's no question there's some global warming, but I'm not sure what it means. A lot of this is condescending elitism."*

That's me; I'm one of those condescending elitists.

If by elitist you mean college educated people who rely on the word of scientists as opposed to Sunday morning preachers who would rather turn the wheel over to Jesus.

But Pat that was not the only time you stuck your oversized foot in your smelly mouth. Remember when you were discussing the American Healthcare Act and a reporter named Alice Olstein asked if you were in favor of removing certain mandated coverage? To which you replied, in superb manner, *"I wouldn't want to lose my mammograms."*

That's genius, Pat.

Pissing on the graves of thousands of mothers, daughters, sisters and wives who lost their lives to breast cancer, just so you could make a cheap joke and score a few political points in the name of Tea Party austerity.

But your bone headedness is legendary and will speak volumes about your time in the Senate long after you have fed the worms.

You were against same sex marriage, no surprise there.

You voted against the Feinstein Amendment, which would have banned suspected terrorists from buying guns. Because, you know, even terrorists have 2nd Amendment rights.

And you were a full-throated supporter of the Patriot Act, giving the president authority for warrantless surveillance, except maybe when the president is black and he's trying to fend off Russian intervention in our elections. We can't have that.

Let's also talk about what you didn't do.

For instance, remember when Precedent Shitgibbon could not take time from his busy day, making phone calls and eating KFC, to visit the Arlington Cemetery? On Veteran's Day? You, a former Captain in the US Marines, said nothing.

Semper Fi -- Always faithful. Well, almost always, right Pat?

One last item I noticed on your Wikipedia page that your birthday is April 20. I'm sure you're not aware of this, but 4/20 is not only a day revered by marijuana aficionados. It also happens to be Adolf Hitler's birthday.

There can be no doubt as to which way your sentiments lean.

Best,

Rich Siegel
siegelrich@mac.com
Culver City, CA 90232

Chapter 44: Senator Mike Rounds
The Round Mound of Duck Down

1.16.19

Senator Mike Rounds
Hart Senate Office Building, Suite 502
Washington, DC 20510

Dear Senator Rounds,

Consider yourself lucky. Very lucky.

You see there's a good chance, owing to your anonymity and complete lack of charisma, you could have been the last letter in my personal campaign to write to each and every Republican Senator. As it is you're number 42.

Let's face it, there's no joy bringing up the rear. But at least you can go to bed at night and sleep fitfully knowing you did not come in dead last.

The irony is, you're indebted to a Democratic colleague for having been spared that shame. Because last week when Precedent Shitgibbon (Mean Girl #1) mocked Senator Elizabeth Warren, you made it known that his tweets were harmful to South Dakota Native Americans who might have lost ancestors at the battle of Bighorn and Wounded Knee.

It was then, and only then, that 330 million Americans ever heard of you.

By the way, why do you go by Mike, and not your given name, Marion?

Homophobe says what?

Anyway, I've looked over your stunning record of standard Republican do nothing-ness and discovered you graduated from South Dakota State University, home of the Jackrabbits. In light of your cookie cutter incompetence, and to honor the mascot of your beloved alma mater, I thought it would be far more interesting to go down the SDSU Jackrabbit hole.

For instance, if you were to walk onto the SDSU campus you'd stumble across the Daschle Research Library, named after former US Senate Majority Leader Tom Daschle. A Democrat.

That's gotta sting, doesn't it, Marion?

Going even further into the jackrabbit hole, did you know that your alma mater was also the home of Gene Amdahl, father of Amdahl's Law?

For the uninitiated, this is one of the pillars of modern day computer architecture.

Evolution according to Amdahl's law of the theoretical speedup is latency of the execution of a program in function of the number of processors executing it. The speedup is limited by the serial part of the program. For example, if 95% of the program can be parallelized, the theoretical maximum speedup using parallel computing would be 20 times.

I don't want to get all geeky on you, but early in my career, I wrote advertising for Apple computers. So I can hold my own in a discussion about parallel processing, sequential transformation and of course, manually confibulated flick flacks.

MR. SIEGEL WRITES TO WASHINGTON

Suffice to say that when the next plaque at SDSU is embossed it'll probably bear Gene Amdahl's name and not yours.

I'm not sure what the college regents have in mind for you.

What do you do for the man who sought to eliminate a woman's right to choose?

Or offered green cards to foreigners in exchange for shady investments in South Dakota beef processing plants? Mmmmm, beef.

Or opposed any legislation regarding the 3-D printing of handguns? Mmmm, guns.

Let's not ignore your stalwart support and leadership in Ducks Unlimited, an organization *"committed to the conservation of wetlands and associated upland habitats for waterfowl, other wildlife."*

Mostly so you can kill them, let's be honest. Hey, there's an idea.

What about The Marion Rounds Memorial Duck Blind. A lasting testament to your deceitfulness, predatory inclinations and your homespun lack of vision.

Best regards,

Rich Siegel
siegelrich@mac.com
Culver City, CA 90232

131

Chapter 45: Senator Mitt Romney
Our Great White Dope

1.24.19

Senator Mitt Romney
B33 Russell Senate Office Building
Washington, DC 20510

Dear Senator Romney,

Welcome to the US Senate.

About a year ago I started writing letters to all the US Republican
Senators. If I'm being completely honest, the task has been
depressing and tedious.

You see, week after week I would hunt down my next victim.
Research their bumbling escapades on the Internet. Dip my pen in
the bottomless well of rage ink and let loose a flurry of fiery
invective on these beslubbering, sodden-witted cullions.

Oh sure, it's fun to uncork the volcano, but as the sadistic guards at
any Turkish prison will tell you, "Sometimes it just gets old." Or,
"bazen sadece yaşlanır."

So you can imagine how refreshing it feels to welcome you to the
Upper Chamber.

MR. SIEGEL WRITES TO WASHINGTON

I'd like to thank the people of Utah for sending us an old guard Republican who believes in fiscal conservatism, global trade, and the institutions of democracy as well as our precious Rule of Law.

It's my hope that as a former presidential candidate you will have the fortitude, the intelligence and the political capitol to stand up to the useful Manchurian idiot who currently watches TV and scarfs buckets of greasy fast food at 1600 Pennsylvania Ave.

Unlike your cowering colleagues who walk on eggshells and fear being at the wrong end of a sniping 280 character tweet.

My plan is to assemble this collection of letters and publish them in a book several months from now.

But I might be looking at this through rose-colored glasses. And ignoring the crumbling precipice we are all standing on. Who's to say we will all be here will be several months from now?

As I write this, the American government is closed for business, the national debt is soaring, the stock market is volatile and the Mueller Report appears to be ready to blow.

You Mitt, and it seems you alone, can save us from a certain catastrophic fall into this horrible abyss...oh wait, I'm being handed a bulletin.

It seems you voted for easing sanctions on our Russian overlords.

And you blamed the #TrumpShutdown on the Democrats.

Oh for Christ's sake (or whatever deity you Mormons pray to.)

Now I don't blame your niece Ronna, the current chair of the RNC, for dropping the Romney name like a Taco Bell Meat Torpedo.

I didn't think it was possible, but you make Jeff Flake look good.

Best regards,

Rich Siegel
siegelrich@mac.com
Culver City, CA 90232

Chapter 46: Senator James Risch
The Weasel on the Hill

2.7.19

Senator James Risch
SR-483 Russell Senate Office Building
Washington, DC 20510

Dear Senator Risch,

I know you.

I recognize you from the Senate Intelligence Hearings, an oxymoron, to say the least.

I can't believe it has taken me this long to get to you. I'm now at the tail end of my list of Republican Senators, to whom I've been handwriting letters. I still have Kramer, Young, Hawley, and those other faceless imbeciles no one has ever heard of.

But I could pick your weaselly face out of any crowd.

You are a man of some import.

If ever there was a Republican Senator who towed the GOP company line with glee and aplomb it would be you. I'll bet you have walk-on privileges at any number of Trump golf courses.

RICH SIEGEL

"You need a tee time, Senator Risch? Let me bump these losers off the tee box and get a cart for you right away. Would you like some Trump-branded golf balls™ and a Trump-branded escort girl™ to accompany you on your round today?"

Hell Jim, they should name a whole suite or wing after you at Mara Lago. Frankly, your mastery of the microphone in service of the president's agenda has been nothing less than sterling.

And no one is quicker to come to his defense.

When lifelong diplomats questioned Captain Ouchie Foot's approach to Russia and North Korea, you stood strong. You even broke with the Chair of the Senate Foreign Relations Committee, Bob "Corky" Corker and tossed aside his alarm.

"Well, look, everybody speaks differently. Certainly, I wouldn't say it the same way the president would, and nobody would else would say it exactly the same way either. But...even the president's enemies and his critics acknowledge that he has been tougher than anybody else. So you've got to look at what a person does and not pay nearly as much attention to the rhetoric."

Damn, Senator, that is the Waldorf Astoria of word salads. You sir, have turned obeisance into a fine art.

I think it's fair to say that the Governor of Idaho (home of America's finest Nazis) made the right decision when you were hand picked to replace Senator Larry Craig --he, of airport bathroom stall fame.

MR. SIEGEL WRITES TO WASHINGTON

Larry Craig made a name for himself by spreading his legs wide and greeting fellow jet travellers with their own personal *"arrival gate."*

In essence, you perform the same deferential service for Precedent Shitgibbon.

Only you do it with your pants on.

Best,

Rich Siegel
siegelrich@mac.com
Culver City, CA 90232

Chapter 47: Senator Johnny Isakson
Johnny Apple Polisher

2.21.19

Senator Johnny Isakson
120 Russell Senate Office Building
Washington, DC 20510

Dear Senator Isakson,

I'd like to be the first Californian to congratulate you on winning the John McCain Service to Country Award.

I don't often find myself in agreement with Republican Senators, 44 of whom have received handwritten letters from me this year, but on the topic of National Service, you and I are like two ripe peaches in a Georgia wicker basket.

I believe that following high school, young people should do a year of mandatory service. That can be in the armed forces or the Peace Corps. Hell, I'd be happy to see these kids slap on a yellow vest and clean debris off our highways.

And so Johnny, we are compatriots.

That concludes the niceties portion of this letter.

So, Senator, what do you plan on doing with the plaque handed to you by Cindy McCain?

MR. SIEGEL WRITES TO WASHINGTON

Perhaps it will go on the mantle, wedged between The Golden Bootlicker Service to President Award and the Commemorative Brown Ring Medal you received for years of "inimitable ingratiation."

Let's see, you voted with Captain Ouchie Foot on tax cuts for the wealthy, taking healthcare away from millions of people, relaxing pollution standards and of course, rubberstamping each of his intensely unqualified nominees to positions of power in the cabinet and in the courts.

Can we take a moment and look up Matthew Spencer Peterson on the YouTube?

You stood behind Individual #1 a whopping 127% of the time. I know that seems to defy the law of mathematics and statistics, but that's what makes you an award winner, doesn't it, Johnny?

Pretty soon you are going to have the opportunity to take your lickspittle ways to new heights.

Allow me to elaborate.

As you know, our Commander in Thief has declared a National Emergency. To build his seen-from-space big, beautiful Wall, he plans to divert money from previously approved military construction projects.

That could put you in a bit of a pickle since you are the Chairman of the Senate Committee on Veteran's Affairs.

Which means sometime in the very near future, some Sergeant, who just did two brutal tours in Iraq and one in Syria, will come home and rejoin his family in a cockroach-infested, tin roof barracks.

And that weary soldier, possibly suffering from PTSD, will come before your committee and ask why he and his wife and his 4 year old daughter have to share a bunk with a horde of typhoid-carrying Norwegian tree rats.

This will be your opportunity to follow the lead of your precious bollock-chinned spunkbubble president. Who, at his most recent press conference, expressed no concern that diverting military construction money -- to build the wall -- would delay projects benefitting the troops like base housing, schools and gyms, (saying, and I quote),

"It didn't sound too important to me."

You should try telling that to our returning vets, Johnny.

See how that works, Senator.

Best,

Rich Siegel
siegelrich@mac.com
Culver City, CA 90232

Chapter 48: Senator Todd Young
The Todster

2.28.19

Senator Todd Young
400 Russell Senate Office Building
Washington, DC 20510

Dear Todd,

I probably should be addressing you as 'Dear Senator', but 'Dear Todd' has such a nice pedantic and dismissive ring to it, I just couldn't resist.

As a point of order, I have been handwriting letters to each of our Republican US Senators. I may be mistaken, after doing this for more than a year, but I do believe that as your name indicates, you are the most junior member in the Senate.

I'm 44.

I hope when I'm 46, like you, I can look back at such a distinguished career.

Let's start where every look back on Todd Young starts, 2007. This is when Indiana's Young Republicans -- who now carry the tiki torch for the original Klansman who began in Indiana -- named you *"Southern Man of the Year."*

There's so much irony in that last statement I barely know how to unpack it. If Neil Young (I'm sure no relation) were dead, he'd be spinning in his grave, in his long matted grey hair.

Let me ask you, as Southern Man of the Year, did you receive any special amenities?

* Free Robe Dry Cleaning

* Lighting the Cross Privileges

* Grand Wizard for A Day (Get to wear the green sheets)

"Whoa, whoa, slow down there camper", I can hear you saying. That kind of charged rhetoric and innuendo are completely unfounded. We're in the Trump era, get used to it.

I can even hear you pointing out your membership in the Republican Main Street Partnership, an association of moderate Republicans who advocate a more liberal stance on social issues.

And to be fair, GovTrack noted that you joined more bipartisan bills than any other Senator.

Good for you, Taaaaahdd.

Here's what you didn't do:

When Commander Clack-Dish summarized the racial hatred and violence in Charlottesville and said there were *"very fine people on both sides,"* you said nothing.

And did even less.

MR. SIEGEL WRITES TO WASHINGTON

When Captain Ouchie Foot called the entire continent of Africa *"a bunch of shithole countries,"* you said nothing again.

And, expectedly, did nothing.

When our Tweeter in Chief gleefully gloated about Jussie Smollett but failed to mention the Coast Guard white supremacist that was planning a mass attack on the press and Democratic congressional representatives (the men and women you go to work with each day), you followed suit, and again did nothing.

We are currently governed by an administration that is driven by hate and political divisiveness. And you and the GOP have failed to demonstrate any type of moral leadership.

By doing nothing, you are encouraging everything.

You're a loser, Taaaahhhhhd.

You're the worst kind of Moderate Republican. The silent kind.

Best regards,

Rich Siegel
siegelrich@mac.com
Culver City, CA 90232

Chapter 49: Senator Josh Hawley
Sargent Sunshine

3.7.19

Senator Josh Hawley
B40A Dirksen Senate Office Building
Washington, DC 20510

Dear Senator Hawley,

Bless you Josh. Bless you.

I'm coming towards the end of my yearlong campaign to write a letter to each of our esteemed Republican US Senators. And frankly I thought I'd be running out of steam. Having using up all the good indignation on high profile, miscreant Senators like Graham and Grassley and McConnell.

To be even more frank, I thought at this point in the juncture I'd be scouring through backwoods newspapers like the Arkansas Argonaut or the West Virginia Pennysaver in search of anything remotely unsavory about your sorry lot, just to get across the finish line.

But then you showed up.

And showed up in such a big way.

Last week, you made national headlines. The Big Show. You were on the main ticket. And that's no small feat considering the numerous debacles that competed for our attention: the Michael Cohen testimony (on 3 separate congressional committees no less), the complete cave-in to North Korea's Dear Eater and the collapse of

144

the denuclearization talks, and Captain Ouchie Foot's two hour grievance-polluzza at CPAC.

Undaunted by all this hoo-ha, you managed to snag some digital ink for yourself. Or, in the popular vernacular: Nevertheless, he persisted.

Allow me to fill the reader in.

For two weeks, marshals had been attempting to serve you with a subpoena and compel you to turn over evidence for some ongoing litigation. But, being of the GOP stripe and reptilian by nature, you managed to slip their grasp.

Temporarily.

This is where it gets juicy. Following your well-publicized appearance at CPAC -- America's favorite gathering of tin foil hat wearers and collectors of Nazi memorabilia -- and just as you were walking off the stage, you got served.

Damn, talk about getting cock blocked?

I bet you were ready to put on your Alex Jones muscle shirt and slam some shots of Jaeger with your armband brothers just to work off the adrenaline. Instead, you had to speed dial your attorneys and start working on Stage II of Operation Obfuscation.

I'm sure no one reading this has any idea why you might be in hot water with Johnny Law.

Let's fix that shall we?

RICH SIEGEL

According to many articles in the Kansas City Star (who am I kidding, I only read one article, after all I'm not some lawyer I'm just some poor schmuck making fun of Republican Senators and we all know how easy that is) you violated the state's Sunshine Laws while campaigning for office.

More specifically, while you were the Attorney General, the state's chief law enforcement officer, you found a way to communicate with your campaign staff in a way that would avoid scrutiny by any investigators or journalists.

How did you do this, Mr. Hardcore Republican, Federalist Society member who often used the Hillary Clinton cudgel to bash his opponent?

You willingly set up a private server and conspired to hide and destroy incriminating emails.

Good night nurse, are you kidding me Joshy?

The God of Political Irony shall forever be in your debt.

Best,

Rich Siegel
siegelrich@mac.com
Culver City, CA 90232

Chapter 50: Senator Kevin Cramer
The Professor

3.14.19

Senator Kevin Cramer
B40C Dirksen Senate Office Building
Washington, DC 20510

Dear Senator Cramer,

"To me, it's a lot to do about nothing," Senator Cramer said of the Michael Cohen hearing before the House Oversight Committee.

Well, look at the big brain on Kevin.

What do they put in that bison meat in North Dakota that turns all its residents into verifiable Mensa genii?

It took me 13 months and about 47 weekly letters to US Republican Senators to finally find one who merits some intellectual respect. Professor Cramerbellum. The Albert Einstein of the Plain States.

I probably shouldn't tangle with a graduate from Concordia College in Morehead, Minnesota. And God knows I'd be a fool to mess with someone who has a Master's Degree from the University of Mary in Bismarck, but I'm a headstrong kind of fella.

A lot to do about nothing, Kev?

The man who was the personal attorney and official "fixer" for our Indelicate JizzTrumpet, testifies with first hand knowledge of bank fraud, tax fraud, insurance fraud, hush money and election fraud, and it's a lot to do about nothing?

But, as you and your brain dead colleagues have so astutely pointed out, Cohen's a liar. A confirmed, scurrilous, conniving, oily-palmed liar.

Yes, and he sat at the right hand of Chief Tongue Shaped Like Fork for more than a dozen years!

Either our president was complicit in that myriad of illicit activities. Or, and I don't know if you or any of you in the Senate have considered this, he is the worst judge of character of any human being that has ever taken a breath of oxygen in the entire history of mankind.

And by the way, if it's the latter, he's also the same man we have entrusted with our national security and who is conducting closed door, one-on-one, secret negotiations with Xi Jinping, Kim Jung Un and Vladimir Putin.

If there's any doubt how those talks are going we can simply look at the debriefing statements or question the translators. Oh, my bad, there were no debriefing statements and the translators have been sworn to secrecy.

I'm going to go with the assumption that Mr. Cohen was telling the truth and that this was not *"a lot to do about nothing"* as you so eloquently put it.

Why?

MR. SIEGEL WRITES TO WASHINGTON

Well for one thing, he has nothing left to lose. If he were to willfully lie to Congress he would be facing additional time in prison. Moreover, in addition to his oral testimony, Mr. Cohen brought documentation.

He produced financial statements, personal and incriminating notes from Precedent Shitgibbon, as well as canceled checks signed on the Resolute Desk inside the Oval Office for god's sake as reimbursement for the money he paid to silence Stormy Daniels, star of *Pussy Sweat* and *Porking with Pride II* for which she was awarded AVN's Best Oral-to-Anal-to-Oral Boy Girl Award.

I choose to believe Mr. Cohen.

You, on the other hand, choose to trust the man who has told more than 10,000 confirmed lies since swearing to uphold our Constitution.

The same demented schmuck who told us, with a straight face, that noisy windmills cause cancer.

That guy.

Best regards,

Rich Siegel
siegelrich@mac.com
Culver City, CA 90232

Chapter 51: Senator Deb Fischer
Madam Ovary

3.21.19

Senator Deb Fischer
454 Russell Senate Office building
Washington, DC 20510

Dear Senator Fischer,

This morning I am a little beside myself. You see, not long ago I decided to pen a letter to each of the 53 Republican US Senators. Not surprisingly there were very few females on the list. Everyone knows about Senator Susan Collins, she of the wavy voice I cannot listen to.

And of course, there's Senator Murkowski from Alaska, she of the wavy moral compass who likes to talk a big game but often votes otherwise. Or as I like to say, *"Senator Murkowski, now with 27% more Jeff Flake."*

So you can imagine my surprise when I stumbled upon Senator Ernst, Senator Hyde-Smith and now you. That makes FIVE females in the Republican Senate Chamber, you know, if you don't count Ms. Lindsey Graham.

My shock is more than chromosomal.

As with every other senator, I've done a little digging and researched your past as Nebraska's finest. This has become my standard operating procedures with each of your colleagues. And absolutely necessary with the senators who don't get air time on CNN or don't grandstand before the respective committees.

By the way, I know he's not a senator but can one of you guys buy a blazer for Congressman Jim Jordan? I used to buy sport coats for my crazy uncle who lived in a nursing home in Atlantic City. The local Goodwill has a very nice selection.

Last week, you did something very few Republican Senators, ever do. You voiced a contrarian opinion and risked incurring the wrath of Precedent Shitgibbon.

"I am angry by reports that show we have long suspected: former EPA Administrator Scott Pruitt ignored the law to help big refineries at the expense of farmers and ethanol producers. The EPA gave 'hardship exemptions' to profitable refineries, releasing them from their biofuel blending obligations. According to projections, this could cause the ethanol industry to lose billions of gallons in demand."

Good for you for finally putting your foot down. Though it must be noted you only raised your voice when there was possibility of millions of dollars were not coming your state's way. Meaning you had no problem with Mr. Pruitt beforehand?

What could have possibly clued you in to this scoundrel's sleazy ways?

His unjustified first class travel?
His unauthorized use of military transport for personal use?
His generous doling out of raises to staff assistants?
His leased condo from a known lobbyist? (I believe he paid $125 a month)

None of that seemed to bother you?

And while we're questioning the unsavory actions of this now defrocked Cabinet member, has it ever occurred to you, or the sheep sitting to your left and your right, to have another look at the swampy hedgepigs that were also handpicked by Captain Ouchie Foot? I'm not talking about the ones who have already been convicted of crimes and await sentencing with the Special Counsel (Cohen, Flynn, Gates). I'm talking about the taintlickers who serve in the White House as we speak. The list is long and ludicrous.

But I've got my eye on Secretary of Labor Alexander Acosta.

Before he joined the clown cabinet, this scumwaffle was a US Attorney who cut a deal with billionaire Jeffrey Epstein, who just happens to be a close friend of your Dear Leader. Epstein was charged with the rape and assault of many underage girls. But instead of serving a lifetime in prison, Secretary Acosta gifted him the Mara Lago Discount, so he did 13 months of house arrest under electronic supervision.

You've not said *one* word regarding Secretary Acosta.

To summarize:

Wealthy & subsidized Nebraska corn farmers getting screwed -- Not cool
40 underage girls getting assaulted and raped -- Cool

Maybe you need to turn in your Woman Card.

Best,

Rich Siegel
siegelrich@mac.com
Culver City, CA 90232

Chapter 52: Senator John Hoeven
Mr. Potter

3.28.19

Senator John Hoeven
338 Russell Senate Office Building
Washington, DC 20510

Dear Senator Hoeven,

I have a confession to make.

For little more than a year now, I have made it my mission to hand write a letter to every Republican Senator currently serving in the 115th legislative session. It's been an eye-opening and informative adventure.

Because upon turning over each and every stone, the natural habitat of the Republican Senator, it's been made abundantly clear, at least to me, that any simpleton could do a better job. I mean seriously, John, how hard can it be?

You vote Yes on issues that are good for the American people, like: access to healthcare, education, care for the elderly, equal rights for all Americans, sensible immigration laws, environmental protection, fair administration of justice, and a host of other common sense policies.

And you vote No on budgets that increase tax breaks for wealthy fuckers, companies that want to pollute and the real recipients of government welfare, the booming industrial/military complex -- that thing Eisenhower, a Republican, warned us about.

It's kind of a simple binary task, isn't it?

Hell, I could get a Boy Scout from the local Culver City troop to build a two-button contraption for you. You'd simply have to hit the right button when it came time for you to vote.

Truthfully, no one is expecting you to actually write any legislation. Or lead the charge. Or take a stand. Or really do anything that would require any ethical fortitude.

After all, you're just a silver-spoon baby who took over daddy's bank and parlayed that wealth into a political position where you can push people around and, if you play your cards right, get approval for one of those "Cones of Silence" that former EPA Administrator Scott Pruitt had installed in his office.

You need one of those, John. You know, to conduct the super-sensitive and highly confidential business of governing North Dakota.

All of which brings me to my original confession.

I am not the brightest bead in the abacus. I'll be the first to admit it. But it seems every time I turn around to write one of these letters I find a new Senator from the Dakotas. It's as if you guys are breeding like feral cats. Obscenely rich, pasty white, feral cats.

MR. SIEGEL WRITES TO WASHINGTON

I know there are only four of you, but if feels like there are forty. Moreover, that disproportional representation becomes even more absurd when one hits the Google.

My jaw hit the foundation holding up my house when I discovered the population of North Dakota was only 760,077. And the population of South Dakota was slightly more at 882,235.

I can find more people in the parking lot at Dodger Stadium on any given hot summer night. Particularly if Kershaw is pitching.

Call me crazy, but there is something seriously wrong when close to 10% of the Senate is controlled by four low voltage bulbs representing a million and a half not-very-bright people.

Apart from picking you as their Senator, what leads me to believe these people are not very bright?

They live in North and South Dakota.

Best,

Rich Siegel
siegelrich@mac.com
Culver City, CA 90232

Chapter 53: Senator Rick Scott
The Sturgeon General

4.4.19

Senator Rick Scott
716 Hart Senate Office Building
Washington, DC 20510

Dear Senator Scott,

We often hear *God Bless America* at sporting events. We hear it at the end of big dramatic speeches. We even hear it after someone sneezes...well, a variation on it.

I would suggest we don't need to hear it anymore. Because God has already blessed America.

Think about it.

God has already given us a Commander in Chief who is tall, slender (at 239 lbs.), a lover of all people, a truth teller, and, as we will get to in a moment, a stable genius.

Our Big Gulp Cup truly runneth over.

At his side, God has also given us 53 US Republican Senators who do his providential bidding. I've made it my mission to write a letter to each and every one of these men and women who are nothing less than God's warriors on Earth. You are letter #51, but let's remember you are late entry into the Senate.

MR. SIEGEL WRITES TO WASHINGTON

Let us also not be discouraged by that, because God, in all his wisdom, has verily shone his grace on all of us. And by that I mean, last week, you, Senator Rick Scott, a veritable beacon of decency, dedication and dignity, were chosen by our divine leader to spearhead the effort to replace Obamacare.

"Lord, we are not worthy of your love."

What have we done to deserve such grace?

How much bounty can be bequeathed on one people?

Many know that you, along with other stable genius, George W. Bush, were co-owners of the Texas Rangers baseball team. What most people don't realize is that your unmatched business acumen was forged in the world of healthcare.
In 1987, you along with major financing from Citicorp, attempted to buy HCA, Hospital Corporation of America, worth close to 4 billion dollars. The attempt fell short, but you, Rick Scott, determined to find your fortune in the misfortune of others, were undeterred.

And in 1994 you became the CEO of Columbia/HCA, the single largest for-profit healthcare company in America.

Mmmmm, unregulated profit.

That's the kind of single-minded drive, determination and callous capitalism that made this country great. And it's the kind of senatorial leadership we so lack these days.

Oh sure, there might have been the occasional FBI investigation. The fraud. The corruption. The anti-kickback violations. The illegal deals with homecare companies. The false cost reporting. And the pharmaceutical irregularities that resulted in thousands of dollars of under the table payments.

But have we learned nothing over the past year? And the futility of prosecuting these frivolous "process crimes?"

The important thing, and I think you and everyone else in America who owns a red golf cap will agree, is that you have what it takes to turn dialysis into a dollar.

You know how to profit from pancreatic cancer.

You have the gumption to make lemonade out of lymphoma.

That makes you special, Rick.

And because Captain Ouchie Foot has chosen you to spearhead this new spectacular healthcare system that will be the envy of the world, well, that makes us blessed.

Best regards,

Rich Siegel
siegelrich@mac.com
Culver City, CA 90232

Chapter 54: Senator Martha McSally
The Red Baroness

4.18.19

Senator Martha McSally
B40D Dirksen Senate Office Building
Washington, DC 20515

Dear Senator McSally,

Let me start this letter with a sincere thank you for your service.

I have to imagine that people like you, who have served in our military, might be jaded by that. On the other hand, I have never met anyone who does not appreciate a little appreciation. And I believe your 22 years in the Air Force deserves recognition.

Furthermore, you have my respect for not only standing down our enemies, but also standing up for what's right.

You went up against the Department of Defense in a landmark case, McSally v. Rumsfeld (I like the sound of _Anything v. Rumsfeld_) and struck a blow for women's rights, particularly those who were being asked to subjugate themselves while serving in places like Saudi Arabia -- home of Bone Saw Diplomacy.

As if all that weren't enough, you've courageously brought attention to the issue of sexual harassment. As the father of two daughters, I applaud your efforts.

RICH SIEGEL

You make Arizona proud.

All of which begs the question, how can someone as principled as
you, turn a blind eye and a silent mouth to what we see transpiring
with the current administration?

How is it, for instance, you have nothing to say about Robert Kraft, a
friend and patron of your president, who was recently caught up in a
sex trafficking scandal while at a rub 'n tug palace once owned by
Mara Lago member, Cindy Yang, aka Grandma Handjob?

What say you on the matter of Jeffrey Epstein, another friend of
Precedent Shitgibbon, who was convicted of assaulting and raping
40 underage girls? And what about the sweetheart prison deal he
received from former US Attorney Alex Acosta, who now sits in the
White House Cabinet as our current Secretary of Labor?

If you had any balls, you'd be knocking down Acosta's door and
dragging his sorry pencil neck ass out to the street.

And finally, only because it's the most recent example of the fascism
that visited America, there is Herr Trump's ban on transgender
soldiers.

Think about this. One day 13,000 of your fellow soldiers, brothers
and sisters serving in the US military are fit for service. On the front
lines. In faraway places. Ready and willing to make the ultimate
sacrifice for their country -- you know, the one that celebrates
equality.

And the next day, because some hamberder-eating clown makes an
oversized autograph on a big green binder, those dedicated warriors
are unfit for service?

Did they suddenly lose the ability to shoot straight?

MR. SIEGEL WRITES TO WASHINGTON

Did they suddenly forget how to fly a plane?

Did they suddenly draw a blank on the intricacies of command and control communications operations?

No.

They simply became unacceptable because some porn-star banging, truth-mauling, condo-shilling, lard-ass con man woke up one day and said they were.

And you did NOTHING.

That's the thing about principles, McSally. If you have them, they don't show up in spurts like new the next season of *Game of Thrones or Better Call Saul*.

They're there 24/7/365.

Where are your principles, Martha? Are they on hiatus?

Best regards,

Rich Siegel
siegelrich@mac.com
Culver City, CA 90232

Chapter 55: Senator Rob Portman
The Blind Buckeye

4.25.19

Senator Rob Portman
448 Russell Senate Office Building
Washington, DC 20510

Dear Senator Portman,

I may be a Wheel of Fortune Whiz Kid in a room full of Jeopardy Tournament Champions, but when it comes to smarts, you sir give Louie Gohmert and Devin Nunes a run for the money.

I'll get to my point as soon as I explain that you are letter #53 in a series of hand written missives to GOP Senators I started more than a year ago. I am certainly glad I waited until this week to address the junior senator from Ohio. Because this week you took a rightful seat next to other cretinous luminaries in the halls of Congress.

Of course, I am referring to Precedent Shitgibbon's latest nomination to the Federal Reserve Board, the accomplished economist and CNN panel punching bag Steven Moore. A man so clueless and lacking in wits that he once said...

"You want to live in Chicago. You don't want to live in Cincinnati or Cleveland or these armpits of America like that."

Like I said, I may be a few peas short of a casserole, but to my fuzzy recollection, those two cities are in your state of Ohio. You would think those would be fighting words, wouldn't you Rob?

MR. SIEGEL WRITES TO WASHINGTON

I'll bet if some dingleberry called Trenton the hairy asshole of North America, Chris Christie would bound from his chaise lounge, douse the offender with tangy BBQ sauce and gobble that poor bastard up as a pre-meal appetizer.

But you? You said nothing. Not one word. Where's your home state pride?

In fact when a reporter pressed you on the issue, you handed it off to one of your spokes-pieholes, who muttered, *"Moore's statement isn't great."*

Want to hear some more not-so-great statements from Mr. Moore? Today's NY Times has a bevy of them. Like this gem...

"There's a new oppressed minority on college campuses these days and it is not women, blacks, Latinos or gays....No, the group that has fallen into great disfavor is the white male."

Yes, because soon white males will not be 95% of the CEOs of America's Fortune 500. Soon that number will drop to a perilous 94%. Think of the devastating effect that will have on our country.

Want more Moore?

With regards to women and basketball, *"Here's the rule change I propose: No more women refs, no women announcers, no women beer vendors, no women anything. There is, of course, an exception to the rule. Women are permitted to participate, if and only if, they look like Bonnie Bernstein."*

I took the liberty of Googling Ms. Bernstein and can safely say she would have nothing to do with a man who apparently gets his hair cut at PetSmart.

Finally, one more from Mr. Bore.

"No one seems to care much that co-ed sports is doing irreparable harm to the psyche of America's little boys."

In this respect he may correct, as evidenced by Steven Moore and the entire tribe of Trump troglodytes, it appears America's little boys never grow up and stop being America's little boys.

And so, being the little spineless toady you are, there's a good chance none of this will have any effect on you and, like you have in the past, will vote along the lines of your bully president. You wouldn't want him tweeting something mean about you.

Or your state's armpit cities.

In short, Rob, you're going to approve Moore to the Federal Reserve Board.
Which impossibly, leaves me thinking even less of you.

Best regards,

Rich Siegel
siegelrich@mac.com
Culver City, CA 90232

Chapter 56: Senator Mike Enzi

4.25.19

Senator Mike Enzi
379A Senate Russell Office Building
Washington, DC 20510

Dear Senator Enzi,

A little more than a year ago, I set out on a mission to hand write a letter to every GOP Senator. You are letter number 56.

I looked into your storied career as Wyoming's proudest...aw, fuck it, you're not even worth the effort...

Best,

Rich Siegel
siegelrich@mac.com
Culver City, CA 90232

Chapter 57: Senator Marsha Blackburn
The Duchess of Dumb

4. 9.19

Senator Marsha Blackburn
357 Dirksen Senate Office Building
Washington, DC 20510

Dear Senator Blackburn,

Marsha. Marsha. Marsha.

Is this an amazing time in American history or what? For the past 52+ weeks, I have been writing letters to every GOP Senator, or as I call them, The Vichy Enablers.

But this week is special, because prior to this writing we only had one rotten scumbag in the Executive wing worthy of impeachment. Now, with the addition of Attorney General Bill Barr, we have two. Two fat, doughy white men marching our great country down the path to authoritarianism.

You'd think a smart woman like yourself --a graduate of Mississippi State University, no less, home of the Fighting Klansmen -- would see the collapse of our great republic as it happens before our eyes and intercede. But you'd be wrong.

Enough about you, let's talk about me.

MR. SIEGEL WRITES TO WASHINGTON

I've been married for more than 387 years. Correction, my wife informs me it's only been 26. And therein lies my point. You see I've come to understand women are great at seeing through men's bullshit. It's an amazing talent that must be attached to the Y chromosome.

For instance, my wife knows when I haven't squeegeed the glass door after a shower. She knows when I haven't walked the dog. She knows when I'm lying about taking out the garbage and can somehow smell under the sink even when she's 293 miles away visiting her sister in Northern California.

She knows. And she lets me know, she knows.

As if there were not enough oppressive estrogen in my life, I have two grown daughters. In fact the youngest is graduating college today. They too have been blessed with EBSP, Extra Bullshit Sensory Perception.

Their protestations, as you might expect, are less about domestic issues and revolve more around cultural and social norms.

For instance, my youngest daughter informs me that my daily weightlifting routine is a lingering remnant of "Toxic White Masculinity." I point out, as many of your Confederate-loving constituents might, that as a member of the Hebrew Tribe, there are many circles that do not consider me white.

Similarly, my girls have vocal opinions on my consumption of red meat, my obsession with football and my tendency to reach for the pause button on the remote control whenever there is a wide shot of the NFL cheerleaders.

The point is the women in my life are astute, mature and committed to improving this world. In other words, everything you are not.

RICH SIEGEL

When asked about the rift between Robert Mueller and Bill Barr,
you repeated the outright lies of the AG:

*"Attorney General Barr said many of the problems were with how
the media had represented the report. And he cannot control what
the media is going to say."*

That's a lie. And that's a lie about a lie.

I suggest you read the letter again. Mr. Mueller makes no mention of
the media. And seeing how he has remained silent for the past two
years, I don't think he gives a crap about media representation.

All of which leads me to conclude, and I hope my daughters will
forgive me, that you are *"One Dumb Lying Bitch."*

Of course, seeing how you've cozied up to our golf playing, porn star
banging, truth twisting, pussy grabber, there's a good chance you'd
like that.

Best,

Rich Siegel
siegelrich@mac.com
Culver City, CA 90232

Chapter 58: Senator Mike Braun
Brawndo

5.16.19

Senator Mike Braun
374 Russell Senate Office Building
Washington, DC 20510

Dear Senator Braun,

Congratulations, Mike.

A little more than a year ago, I set out on a mission to write a letter to each of the 53 GOP US Senators. The numbers get hazy because some of you were booted out by a disgruntled electorate who discovered the effort to Make America Great Again has become an effort to revive the Fourth Reich.

Along with the senators leaving the chamber, there were a couple of new ones entering. Suffice to say, at this point I have lambasted the entire lot of you.

And guess what? Of all those useless, witless, clueless Trump sycophants, you, Mike, in your magnificent, inimitable fecklessness, have come in dead last.

Let me tell you, having become acquainted with the logger headed antics of Bonehead Boozman, Barasso the Asshole, and Crappy Mike Crapo, that is quite the accomplishment.

RICH SIEGEL

I know it's kind of juvenile and sophomoric to be tossing around 8th grade nicknames, particularly when they are aimed at our elected leaders, but I have to assume that since you've never voiced any objection to our president doing so, you'll have no problem with me picking up the same practice.

Reciprocity. Isn't that one of Precedent Shitgibbon's favorite words?

I'd also like to congratulate myself on some fortuitous timing.

You see, this week you actually made the national news. And did it with the inefficacious, fustian flair that has become the Mike Braun signature.

When asked by reporters how your constituents, farmers in the great state of Indiana, were coping with the Chinese trade war, initiated by your own Captain Ouchie Foot, you hemmed, hawed, and blurted out...

"Most farmers have been weaned off of government involvement (socialism), but in the process of dealing with the Chinese, even though I don't like it (socialism) philosophically. We come to help them (socialism) if we are still at an impasse. I really believe with China it's going to take some time (more socialism)."

That's the kind of masterful, cover-all-bases, don't-upset-Commander Bunglefart, noncommittal unleadership that will take you far, mister.

Well played sir, well played.

Frankly, I couldn't find a better way to wrap up this effort.

MR. SIEGEL WRITES TO WASHINGTON

Because you, Mike Braun, a know nothing, do nothing, soulless, rock-brained, ribbon-cutting, brownnosing bureaucrat may be the pitch perfect embodiment of a United States Republican Senator.

Thank you for your service, Mike.

Best,

Rich Siegel
siegelrich@mac.com
Culver City, CA 90232

Chapter 59: Senator Mitch McConnell
Kentucky's Worst

6.6.19

Senator Mitch McConnell
317 Russell Senate Office Building
Washington, DC 20510

Dear Mitch,

It's been a while since our last correspondence. Actually it's been more than a year.

Unlike you, who have done nothing but obstruct House bills, defend our indefensible precedent (misspelling intentional for dramatic effect) and nominate halfwits to be federal judges (Matthew Spencer Peterson) I have been quite busy.

As I mentioned in a previous dispatch, I made it my mission to write a letter to each of our esteemed GOP senators. At the beginning of the endeavor there were 51 of you utter clay-brained pignuts.

But that number has changed.

Some of your colleagues went down to defeat in Red Wave 2018 (pffft).

Some new fresh faces have entered the fold, ready to take their place at the Mitch McConnell Trough of Eternal Corruption.

And some, if I'm not mistaken, were arrested and hauled off for a jumpsuit fitting at a local correctional facility, charged with pedophilia, sex trafficking and handing raw polling data over to Russian intelligence officers.

Oh, I apologize, those weren't US Senators, those were members of the president's inner circle.

Sometimes it's difficult to tell the duly elected slimebags from the ones who were appointed by our Loutish, Shrill-Gorged Gudgeon.

Truth be told --a phrase I'm not sure you're familiar with -- it's been quite an enlightening adventure.

Prior to 2016, I considered myself politically engaged and informed. But in the process of researching you, and all of your criminal co-conspirators, I discovered I was sorely lacking in any understanding of civics as well as the role of the Upper Chamber, or what President James Buchanan, with tongue piercing his cheek, called, *"the greatest deliberative body in the world."*

The US Senate is more accurately where old white millionaires go to bone naive but ambitious Washington interns and slither around in loosely draped threadbare towels in the taxpayer-funded schvitz room in the Capitol building basement. -- *The Lindsey Graham Sweatorium,* I'm told it's called.

Images, that require copious amounts of eyewash.

The first thing I learned, I should say "we learned" as in each of the letters has been dutifully published on my daily blog roundseveneteen.blogspot.com and enjoyed by 20,000 monthly readers, is that so many senators sport eponymous names.

Crapo, Boozman and Sasse (Sassehole), immediately come to mind. I know that's immature and crass, but judging from who you put in the White House, those are winning attributes.

We've also learned that the Republican Party, which once planted and saluted the flag of Family Values, has cashed in that losing platform. It could be Captain Ouchie Foot is threatening you or paying you or possibly both, but there can be no doubt that the 115th Congress has a brand, new playbook.

And it was published by the fine people at Trump University, who also brought us *101 Ways to Finance that Condo in Boca Raton* and *The Art of Dodging Contractors*.

While I haven't seen this new barbarous GOP Manual, I can safely surmise some of the groundbreaking new principles:

1. **We are adamantly Pro Life**-- Except if the people living those lives are from countries other than Norway and their skin is brown. Then we're all about extracting babies from their mothers, depositing them in hot wire cages and losing all records that might possibly reunite them with their families. Just as Jesus commanded in Two Corinthians.

2. **We are adamantly Pro Constitution**-- Nothing is as important to the future of our republic as the adherence to the Rule of Law. And respect for those officials who are sworn to law enforcement. Except when they are investigating Russian interference in our election. Or when overzealous congressional bodies issue subpoenas and cavort with overreaching judges to question our divinely chosen King...er, president.

3. **We are adamantly Pro Military**-- The country owes an incalculable debt to the brave men and women who serve in our armed services and are true heroes. Except those who are taken prisoner behind enemy lines. *"We like heroes who don't get caught."*

174

MR. SIEGEL WRITES TO WASHINGTON

And though we honor our warrior's past, present and future, we have second thoughts about the 407,931 soldiers who died in World War II fighting Nazis and fascism, which in the cleansing light of history we now believe have been maligned. After all they were *"very fine people."*

From a more micro perspective and, thanks to my weekly research into each of you 53 scoundrels, I learned of the many peccadilloes that make you Republicans tick.

Like the honorable Senator David Perdue who shamelessly toiled as a corporate raider, fleeced companies, scurried off with the liquid assets and then unceremoniously stood by while thousands of his fellow Georgians lost their jobs.

Who can forget Senator Jim Inhofe, the Mensa of the Senate, who, eager to disprove the Chinese-fabricated hoax of global warming, brought a real live snowball into the Chamber? If ever there was definitive proof that 97% of the world's top scientists and climate experts were simply dead wrong with all their data and research and examples of reproducible scientific findings, it was this 84-year-old yahoo from Oklahoma, holding a fistful of dirty DC slush.

Finally, how can we ignore Aunt Pity Patty, Ms. Lindsey Graham? Who at one time called our Great Unschooled Wanker, *"xenophobic"*, *"a kook"* and *"unfit for office."* He's gone from being a Never Trumper to an Always Trumper, seemingly taking up permanent residence in the president's KFC-encrusted alimentary canal.

And you Mitch have the honor of presiding over and leading these impudent scullions. Whipping them into shape and insisting they enable and promote the most corrupt, ill informed, destructive, impulsive and foreign-manipulated presidency in the history of western civilization.

When future scholars look back on how this regime has damaged the republic, they will wear out the letters T-R-U-M-P on their keyboards.

I suspect the letter M will go first because you, Mitch McConnell, were a willing and eager accomplice.

Think about that, for all of eternity, you, your reputation, and indeed your family's legacy, shall forever be tied at the hip to this two-bit, shabby, unlettered, uncultured, unwitting condo pimp.

Let me leave you with one last thought.

Mind you this is not something I would ever commit to print in the BT (Before Trump) era. But now that political discourse has sunk lower than the foundation of an unfinished Trump hotel in Uruguay, I have no qualms sinking to the depths you Republicans have been accustomed to.

When you no longer breath the oxygen that is better suited for human beings and pond slugs, I plan to make a 2178-mile pilgrimage to your home state. I will wait for a dark and rainy day, when visitors and security guards would prefer to stay inside.

Then, I will visit you in your final resting place. I will leave a signed copy of this book (a compilation of all my letters) beside your tombstone.

And in an act of civil disobedience as well as a homage to my hero, Gerard Finneran, I will also take the time to "fertilize" the rich Kentucky bluegrass that forever blankets your memory.

You're welcome.

Rich Siegel
siegelrich@mac.com
Culver City, CA 90232

Chapter 60: Senator Lindsey Graham
Aunt Pity Patty

8.9.19

Senator Lindsey Graham
290 Russell Senate Office Building
Washington, DC 20510

Dear Senator Graham,

I owe you an apology.

I recently published a new book entitled Mr. Siegel Writes to Washington, wherein I wrote letters to each of the GOP US Senators. Perhaps clouded by the nonstop flow of presidentially-induced rage, I somehow tripped over myself and forgot to include you.

More likely, I was pacing myself.

You know getting the no-name Senators like Enzi, Hawley and Hoeven, out of the way. And saving my energy for the big fish like you.

In any case, the first edition of the book has turned out to be an abridged version.

You sir, will appear in the second.

Because a proper dressing down of Senate GOP would not be complete without the inclusion of the most traitorous, most obsequious, most repugnant Republican who has ever crossed the threshold at the Russell Senate Office Building -- that would be you, Aunt Pity Patty.

At this point it seems redundant to rehash all the debacles of the last two years.

Like how you went from being a Never Trumper to an Always Trumper.

Or how you preen in front of the camera making a big stink about proper presidential behavior and Russian sanctions and "smoking bone saws."

That's just you, flapping your loose Carolina jaw.

Besides after spending an eternity in the Congress, both as a House Representative and as a Senator, I suspect your skin is tougher than the hindquarter of an old armadillo.

There's nothing this smart ass Jew from New York can say that will leave a mark.

But there is someone you might still respect, someone whose thoughts and actions and deeds might still resonate, as they still do for a once great nation.

MR. SIEGEL WRITES TO WASHINGTON

"Glory belongs to the act of being constant to something greater than yourself, to a cause, to your principles, to the people on whom you rely and who rely on you."

-- Senator John McCain

Any of that ring a bell, Senator?

Or did your honor go into the ground with your late lifetime friend?

Best,

Rich Siegel
siegelrich@mac.com
Culver City, CA 90232

ACKNOWLEDGEMENTS

At this point, many authors go to the trouble of writing one last paragraph in order to recognize all the people who helped. I don't know why I'm going to that trouble as I'm less of a real author and more of just a really pissed off advertising copywriter.

Nevertheless, there were many who helped and made this book possible. I'll list them here so the CIA can immediately add them to their enemy's list.

Jean Robaire and Rohitash Ro, for providing me with a slew of book cover design options.

The final selection was my way of serving notice to right wingers who believe they have some kind of unearned monopoly on patriotism. They don't.

Love of country means participating in this grand experiment we call democracy. It means standing up for the principles that made our forefathers worthy of admiration; noble concepts like equality, liberty, and free thought.

Patriotism is not about sporting red golf caps, wearing a lapel pin or plopping your fat ass down on a shoddy, Chinese-made beach towel silkscreened to look like a US flag.

I also want to thank the readers of my blog, roundseventeen.blogspot.com. Their faint encouragement and preferred loyalty to George Tannenbaum and his blog adaged.com continue to dispirit me and keep me striving to do better.

I must also acknowledge my family. I want to thank my daughters for never reading a word I write, which also means they never critique a word I write.

And I want to thank my wife, Debbie, who, while not laughing at all my jokes anymore, has also developed an amazing tolerance for being around me.

There are many days when I wake up and dread the thought of spending the next 16-17 hours with myself. Yet she has done it for 3 decades. Year in and year out. Day in and day out. And never ever raising her voice or lodging a complaint.

Well, almost never.

ABOUT THE AUTHOR

Rich Siegel is the author of *Tuesdays With Mantu, My Adventures with a Nigerian Con Artist. Round Seventeen & 1/2, The Names Have Been Changed to Protect the Inefficient. And The Big Book of Rants.*

Rich blogs regularly at http://roundseventeen.blogspot.com